New Demographics
New Workspace

Office design for the
changing workforce

New Demographics
New Workspace

Office design for the
changing workforce

Jeremy Myerson, Jo-Anne Bichard and Alma Erlich

Routledge
Taylor & Francis Group

LONDON AND NEW YORK

First published in paperback 2024

First published 2010 by Gower Publishing

Published 2016 by Routledge
4 Park Square, Milton Park, Abingdon, Oxon OX14 4RN

and by Routledge
605 Third Avenue, New York, NY 10158

Routledge is an imprint of the Taylor & Francis Group, an informa business

British Library Cataloguing in Publication Data
Myerson, Jeremy. -
    New demographics, new workspace : office design for the changing workforce. -
        1. Office layout. 2. Work environment. 3. Design--Human factors. 4. Knowledge workers--Case studies. 5. Older people--Employment--Case studies. -
    I. Title II. Bichard, Jo-Anne. III. Erlich, Alma. -
    658.2'3'0844-dc22 --

Library of Congress Cataloging-in-Publication Data
Myerson, Jeremy.
    New demographics, new workspace : office design for the changing workforce / by Jeremy Myerson, Jo-Anne Bichard, and Alma Erlich.
        p. cm.
    Includes bibliographical references and index.
    ISBN 978-0-566-08854-4(hardback)
    1. Office layout. 2. Work environment. 3. Design--Human factors. 4. Older people--Employment. 5. Knowledge workers--Case studies. 6. Older people--Employment--Case studies. I. Bichard, Jo-Anne. II. Erlich, Alma. III. Title.
    HF5547.2.M94 2010
    658.2'3--dc22

                                                                                2010005759

    ISBN: 978-0-566-08854-4 (hbk)
    ISBN: 978-1-03-283815-1 (pbk)
    ISBN: 978-1-315-59792-8 (ebk)

DOI: 10.4324/9781315597928

Contents

About the Authors   *ix*
Acknowledgements   *xi*

Preface   **1**

Part One   **Reviewing the context**

1   **The change we face**   **6**
                 A different workplace   7
                 Knowledge to the fore   8
                 Office design as a priority   9

2   **The greying workforce**   **11**
                 Britain's demographic change   13
                 A global picture of ageing   14
                 Australia follows the age curve   15
                 Policy as a panacea   15
                 International responses to the problem   17

3   **Knowledge workers**   **18**
                 Quantifying the output   19
                 Clueless about working conditions   20
                 What we know about knowledge workers   21
                 Fad, fashion and faith in redesign   22
                 Technology gets in the way   23
                 New ideas are needed   24

4   **Burned-out, bottlenecked and bored**   **25**
                 Options to revitalise careers   26
                 Survivors, jugglers and choosers   27

Work Ability in Finland | 28
Capturing design requirements | 29
Devising a design agenda | 31

5 | An unholy alliance | 32
Work ethic and aesthetic | 33
Giant pieces of engineering | 33
Making pseudo-science visible | 35

6 | Collaborative working | 36
Satisfaction enhances productivity | 37
Segmentation and choice | 38
The rise of open plan | 39
Problems with open plan | 40

7 | Flexible working | 42
The networked office | 43
Working across locations | 44
Do novelties work? | 45

8 | The nature of the challenge | 47
Inclusive design movement | 47
Reacting against one-size-fits-all | 48
An onus on the employer | 49
Physical requirements | 49
How to sustain well-being | 50
Why user context matters | 51

Part Two | Rethinking the culture

9 | Towards a welcoming workplace | 54
A multidisciplinary approach | 55
Three global knowledge industries | 56
How the study was undertaken | 57

10 | Open plan has its limits | 59
A deliberate plan to network | 60
Collaboration versus concentration | 61
Escaping to the home | 62
Hot-desking is a hot issue | 63

	Mapping out the provision of space	64
	A problem with confidentiality	65
11	**Fit for purpose?**	**67**
	A need for alternatives	68
	Problems with shared space	69
	Rest and recuperation	70
12	**Trapped inside the box**	**72**
	Staying abreast of technological change	73
	Struggles with self-sufficiency	74
	Must technology always be the answer?	77
	Alternatives to the screen	78
	Productivity not optimised	79
13	**Ambivalence to ageing**	**80**
	Past culls cast a shadow	81
	Stereotypes shape relationships	83
	No special thought for ageing	84
	Where inclusive design fits in	85
14	**Responding to the challenge**	**86**
Part Three	**Redesigning the environment**	
15	**Plotting your moves**	**90**
	Do big corporate offices have a future?	90
	Environmental changes make a difference	91
	Acoustics, lighting and technology	93
	Response to furniture interventions	95
	Provocations for design change	96
	Three generic types of workplace	98
16	**Spaces to concentrate**	**99**
	Lighting as a lever to concentrate	100
	Choosing furniture for focus	101
	Reaching an optimal experience	102
	Workspace design and the state of flow	104
	Understanding our place in the process	105
	Principles of space for concentration	106

17	**Spaces to collaborate**	**108**
	Planning for teamwork	109
	Reaping dividends from project space	109
	Creating innovation hubs	110
	Breaking down departmental silos	110
	Building a meeting 'tree'	112
	The giant whiteboard	113
	Project rooms promoted	114
	Does brainstorming really work?	116
	Making open plan work for innovation	116
	Missing the point on teamwork	118
	Principles of space for collaboration	118
18	**Spaces to contemplate**	**120**
	When breakout means a break	121
	Taking cues from domestic space	122
	Allowing creativity to flourish	124
	Making people happier	125
	Principles of space for contemplation	126
19	**Making it happen**	**128**
	A range of settings	128
	Addressing the key issues	129
	Breaking with the past	130
20	**New demographics, new workspace**	**134**
	References	*136*
	Index	*140*

About the Authors

Jeremy Myerson is the Helen Hamlyn Professor of Design at the Royal College of Art, where he leads the Helen Hamlyn Centre. A journalist, academic and design activist, he was the Founding Editor of Design Week and he also established InnovationRCA, an innovation network for business. He is the author of a number of books on workplace design, including *New Workspace New Culture* for Gower, and lectures and consults internationally on the subject.

Jo-Anne Bichard is a Research Fellow in the Royal College of Art's Helen Hamlyn Centre. She trained as a social anthropologist at Goldsmiths College and her MSc at Imperial College involved an ethnographic study of neuroscience laboratories. Her research focus is on barriers to and opportunities for inclusive design of products and environments, including the workplace.

Alma Erlich is a Chartered Psychologist with 20 years experience of consulting to organisations, providing management development, evaluation, training and coaching to senior management. Alma is a Consultant to the Royal College of Art Helen Hamlyn Centre, advising on research for design innovation and workplace environments. She is also a Member of the British Psychological Society, the Association of Business Psychologists and the Social Research Association.

Acknowledgements

The authors would like to thank the many organisations and individuals who have contributed to the writing of this book. It has truly been a collaborative experience. We therefore thank: our researchers Catherine Greene and Matthew Harrison at the Helen Hamlyn Centre, Royal College of Art, for their creative insights and ideas; Dr John Smith at JSA Architecture for architectural advice; Margaret Durkan for her communication support; sharp-witted cartoonist Roger Beale of the *Financial Times*; those knowledge workers and company experts who participated in field studies in London, Yokohama and Melbourne as part of the *Welcoming Workplace* study that forms the centrepiece of this book; industry partners DEGW, Steelcase, Colebrook Bosson Saunders, Cordless Group, Kinnarps, Logitec and Future Acoustic for supporting the design interventions at business sites; academic partners Professor Yasuyuki Hirai and Dr Atsue Takeoka at the University of Kyushu in Japan, and Dr Scott Drake and Lauren Zmood at the University of Melbourne in Australia; Professor Thomas Inns, director of the Designing for the 21st Century programme; and staff and colleagues at the Royal College of Art, in particular Sandra Kemp and Jessica Rana in the RCA Research Office. For more information on the *Welcoming Workplace* study, see www.welcomingworkplace.com

Preface

Offices shape the lives of millions of people. How we plan, design and equip them says a great deal about the culture of organisations, the mentality of managers and the motivations of staff.

Some office design is accidental or unthinking, the result of decisions deferred rather than made. But today companies are generally paying more attention to the design of their workplaces, recognising that new business challenges, new technologies and new ways of working require environments better able to flex and adapt. As a result, office design has become one of the fastest-moving areas of design practice, its landscape constantly altered by managers, architects, designers and estates professionals in a bid to stay abreast of the demands placed upon it by organisational change.

In 1998, I co-authored a book for Gower entitled *New Culture New Workspace* with Gavin Turner. Our book aimed to persuade senior managers in business and government to tear down walls, eradicate bureaucratic structures and remove cultural barriers to create more open work environments. At a time when many companies in the 1990s were introducing change management programmes for employees to cope with volatile business conditions, we argued that such exercises were largely futile unless accompanied by a redesign of the office environment to improve teamwork, communication and morale. We provided a range of conceptual models to assist in that process – from town squares and village neighbourhoods to clubs and campaign rooms.

By the turn of the millennium, many of the more open and collaborative principles that we advocated in *New Culture New Workspace* were being widely adopted by different types of organisation. From city workers to civil servants, there was a gradual shift to open-plan working, first a trickle and then a tide. We felt we'd helped to win the argument about the direct impact of physical conditions on how people work, an issue often overlooked in management. We felt we'd succeeded in getting companies to think in a fresh way about culture and environment rather than imposing the dead hand of process and systems.

But as the new decade wore on and such concepts as 'open innovation' and 'collaborative culture' became buzzwords, I began to recognise that maybe the pendulum was beginning to swing too far in the opposite direction. Maybe the call to break down barriers and introduce a cappuccino culture in every organisation was creating as many discomforts as opportunities. The type of workforce we originally discussed in *New Culture New Workspace* was changing – in terms of demographics and attitude and, crucially, in terms of the type of work being done in an increasingly knowledge-based economy.

Twelve years on from the 1998 publication, this new book is in many ways a sequel. *New Demographics New Workspace* adopts the same three-part structure of the original – reviewing the context and then rethinking the culture and redesigning the environment. Once again a series of new conceptual design models are discussed. *Financial Times* cartoonist Roger Beale, who brings a welcome levity to the serious business of the office environment, again comments wryly on the action.

Whereas *New Culture New Workspace* alerted senior managers to how office design can support changes to organisational culture to enable more effective and fulfilled working lives, this new volume has a modified message – its purpose is to alert senior managers to how the design of the work environment can support an ageing workforce to enjoy an extended working life inside knowledge-based organisations.

My co-author on the first book, Gavin Turner, was an expert in management and marketing; our focus for the most part was on business productivity. To develop this new book, I collaborated with an anthropologist, Jo-Anne Bichard, and a psychologist, Alma Erlich. It is no surprise that a design and architectural writer should seek a partnership with experts in the social sciences given the profound links between work habitat and human behaviour. Our focus for the most part here is on motivating the workforce.

Just as the original book was based partly on an academic study – a De Montfort University review of *The Changing Government Workplace* led by Gavin Turner – so *New Demographics New Workspace* also has an academic research project at its centre. Jo-Anne Bichard and Alma Erlich worked closely with me at the Royal College of Art's Helen Hamlyn Centre on the two-year study *Welcoming Workplace*, funded jointly by two UK research councils, the AHRC and EPSRC, as part of the Designing for the 21st Century initiative. Many of the ideas in this book are based on that study and I wish to pay tribute to my co-authors for their expertise and endeavour.

What I learnt 12 years ago was that office environment and corporate culture are entwined – that physical barriers reinforce mental ones and that territorial imperatives hold up a mirror to the power plays of managers. In 2010, many of the physical barriers that characterised the inflexible and unloved late twentieth century office are gone, but getting the balance right between management efficiency and individual wellbeing is as elusive as ever. *New Demographics New Workspace* looks for answers in some new places.

Jeremy Myerson
London

Part One
Reviewing the context

'What has not sunk in is that a growing number of older people ... will participate in the labour force in many new and different ways'

Peter Drucker, Economist

1   The change we face

An older and wiser workforce will steer the future economy

In the early years of the twenty-first century, the world of work in general, but office work in particular, stands on the brink of transformational change. The skills and qualifications of the workforce, the patterns of working, the technologies and systems in use, the design of places and spaces for work, and the rewards in retirement after work – all of these things are under review at a time of unforeseen instability in global financial markets.

Such dramatic shifts are not unprecedented. Exactly 100 years ago, the workplace was transformed by a series of new industrial technologies, among them the typewriter, telephone, elevator, electric light bulb and adding machine, which helped to create a new environment for working and shaped the template for office life in the twentieth century. Indeed the history of work has been driven by technological change from the spinning jenny to the silicon chip.

The change we face today once again has new technologies at its core – these are the information technologies of the Internet, which are forcing nearly all organisations to rethink and regroup, and accompanying digital devices which make remote and mobile working more feasible. But this time there are crucial differences that suggest social and demographic change rather than technological advance will be the dominant factor in comprehensively reshaping employment and the workplace.

This is because the average age of the twenty-first century workforce will be older than at any time in human history and because the nature of the work these employees will be doing in offices will be more closely related to the production and distribution of knowledge than the production and distribution of goods and services, therefore requiring more emphasis on the individual's know-how, learning and expertise.

A different workplace

The combination of a changing age profile in the workforce and the changing nature of work tasks in the knowledge economy, demanding a higher level of skill and experience, leads the authors of this book to the view that a different type of workplace will be required to accommodate a changing workforce. In place of the paper-shifting office that emerged in the early twentieth century, modelled on the time-and-motion studies of factory floor and geared to the dominant economic model of Taylorism (after Frederick Taylor), one can foresee a new, digitally-driven type of workplace that is more flexible in use of time and space, more welcoming to its workforce, more tolerant of the frailties of ageing and more geared to the needs of knowledge interactions.

In formulating ideas and plans for this new workplace, it can be argued that the study of demographic trends, which can be predicted with a measure of accuracy and confidence, provides a more stable basis to plan for change than either technological trends, which tend to be uneven in their adoption by office-based organisations, or economic ones which currently baffle the brightest minds. It is instructive to recall how few economic commentators were able to predict the global banking crisis before autumn 2008.

In contrast, demographics have a clear-cut, profound and entirely predictable impact on the workplace. We know that population ageing is a worldwide phenomenon due to falling fertility rates, better healthcare and nutrition, early childhood immunisation and improving survival rates from chronic diseases such as cancer. We know that the share of older people over 65 is increasing almost everywhere and that the pensions provision for those retiring from the workplace has been badly damaged by the effect of plummeting share prices on pension funds.

While we enjoy the prospect of longer lives, pushing the limits of human longevity ever upwards, we also know that the ratio of potential workers (aged 15–64) to the over-65s is declining rapidly. This leaves governments worldwide with a major headache in figuring out how to pay for the welfare costs of the elderly with a shrinking workforce in a fiercely competitive global economy. Japan and Europe have the fastest ageing populations – nearly one-third of Japanese citizens will be over 65 by 2030 while one in two European adults of working age will be over the age of 50 by 2020 – but other nations face the same frightening demographic curve.

The scale of the economic challenge to national wealth and prosperity posed by population ageing is unprecedented and exacerbated by corporate early-retirement policies, which have culled a whole generation of older workers, and there are no prior employment models on which to lean. Labour supply shortfalls in previous eras were answered by admitting wider social groups into the workforce, either women or people from outside the nation state. Women are now an established part of the workforce and can no longer be seen as an untapped resource. Immigration meanwhile is still widely regarded as part of the economic answer to a shrinking workforce; within Europe, Spain has managed the highest levels of immigration to meet labour shortages head on. But more economic migrants must today show evidence of qualifications and training as governments calibrate immigration policy more tightly to the needs of the knowledge economy.

Knowledge to the fore

Why have knowledge and information come to the fore so strongly in thinking about the workplace? This is because the new workplace is set to run on creativity and brainpower, not engineering-led processes, and must take its organisational cues from that realisation. Much of the repetitive process work that once occupied large numbers of staff in offices within developed economies is today already handled by computers or sent offshore to lower-cost economies. More organisational time and effort is being spent on what is known as 'knowledge work'. This type of work depends not so much on formula and process, working to a set script within a supervised hierarchy, but on independently applying formal knowledge and learning as part of a culture of collaboration, initiative and innovation.

Knowledge workers present new challenges to how work should be organised. Many sit outside the formal hierarchies of their organisations and work on projects to their own individual timetables, setting their own deadlines and targets. They tend to be self-motivated and reliant on their own experience and expertise to undertake special-assignment or consulting work for their own employers. Clocking on to nine-to-five regimes hold little meaning for them.

Research suggests that knowledge workers identify themselves more with their professional discipline and specialism and less with their employer or place of work. They expect to work in a variety of situations and for a number of employers over their working life. The constant is their knowledge, which they want to keep updated. They require a stronger element of trust and individual control in the workplace and take more personal responsibility for the results of their work. Many knowledge workers are also *de facto* older workers because they have acquired their knowledge and expertise over the course of a long career.

Here two trends collide. The classic, instinctive answer for governments facing a combination of a shrinking workforce and rising age-related welfare costs is to encourage a deferment of retirement – to engineer an extension to working lives in order to plug the knowledge gap with older workers who have gained and honed the necessary know-how over time. Employers who are dismayed to see the 'corporate memory' of the organisation drain away with every retirement party are supportive of such moves, because they are increasingly interested in retaining knowledge and experience within their businesses.

It is not difficult therefore to envisage, in the early decades of the twenty-first century, growing numbers of older office workers who will not retire at the expected age but will remain at work for longer, many of them on a consultancy, special-project or part-time basis. But to encourage such well-qualified, mature staff to choose to stay on after the normal retirement age requires the emergence of a different type of workplace – one in which the design of jobs, work processes, management structures and institutional attitudes to ageing are radically rethought.

Office design as a priority
Some of this is already underway, but it is an inescapable fact that none of the important cultural, contractual or human resource changes envisaged will really count unless a redesign of the physical office setting is given priority within organisational change as an obvious lever for transformation. One needs to consider a redesign of the office environment itself, especially as older knowledge workers are likely to be compromised in the work environment by the inevitable effects of ageing on vision, hearing, posture, memory, balance, muscular strength, dexterity and so on.

Here we reach the central theme this book aims to discuss. If an older and wiser workforce is set to steer the future economy, bridging the talent gap in key areas of knowledge work, what are the optimum workplace design considerations for this changing workforce to succeed? We know that the scientifically managed, one-size-fits-all office environment of the twentieth century neither fits the more unstructured, experiential demands of knowledge work, nor addresses the needs and aspirations of an ageing workforce. But we are struggling to give design shape and form to the new workplace that could replace it.

The picture is complex. It is now possible to walk into an office almost anywhere in the world and find up to four generations at their desks in one space. Any new solutions must therefore accommodate not just the baby boomers but younger colleagues too within an inclusive framework. In the following chapters we examine the contexts for ageing and for knowledge work. The scale of the change we face demands we start finding the right design solutions right now.

2   The greying workforce

Throw a stone in the workplace and you'll hit a senior

To see a workforce greying before your eyes, look east. Creaking under the weight of its own success in boosting longevity, Japan has the world's fastest ageing population. A quarter of its citizens are now aged 65 and over. In less than one lifetime Japan has shifted from a country with a young population to the one with the highest proportion of older people. In 1950 the median age of the Japanese population was just 22 – by 2005 this had climbed to 43. In 2050 the average age will be 55. As a consequence, Japan expects its workforce to shrink by 16 per cent in the next 25 years. Little wonder that when a senior figure in Tokyo's Building Research Institute presented his country's demographic picture, he said simply: 'If you throw a stone in Japan, it will hit a senior.'

Japan's response to this demographic shift has been to encourage older workers to stay in employment for longer. Previously its system of retirement or *teinen* (literally 'prescribed year') designated retirement at the age of 55. On reaching this age, many people (especially men) continued working, many with the company they had been with all their working life. However, in many cases *teinen* meant working at a lower level and with a resulting loss of status and income.

In the 1980s, in response to the growing ageing population, the Japanese Government raised the age of *teinen* to 60, and created 'silver talent centres' in major cities as places where older workers could find employment as well as help with financial concerns. Yet many of the seniors seeking work tended to be educated 'white-collar' workers who were considered overqualified for the menial jobs generally offered to older people, such as cleaning parks or guarding bicycles at train stations.

Today, as the economic position tightens further, Japan is looking to raise its pension payout age from 60 to 65. It may have the most rapidly ageing population but it is not the only nation taking action as a declining workforce puts a strain on public and corporate pensions. In the UK, there has been agitation to raise the official retirement age from 65 to 67 while defined benefit pension schemes are facing closure. A similar picture is emerging in the United States where there are plans to raise the social security retirement age.

Governments around the world have little choice but to consider such actions to avoid taking a massive financial hit in the context of population ageing. In 2008, according to the Stanford Longevity Center, average life expectancy at birth was 82 in Japan, 79 in the UK and 78 in the US. By 2050, it will be 87 in Japan, 84 in the UK and 83 in the US. Worldwide, life expectancy will rise from 67 in 2008 to 75 in 2050 and the percentage of over-60s in the global population will double from 11 per cent to 22 per cent. By 2050, Japan will have greyed to the extent of having 44 per cent of its population over 60, but the UK won't be that far behind: 30 per cent will be over the age of 60.

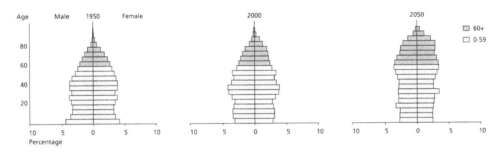

United Nations population pyramids for the UK showing the projected population bulge in the over 60s (United Nations, 2002)

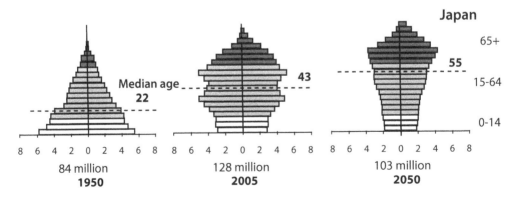

United Nations population pyramids for Japan showing rise in median age (United Nations Revised Stanford Longevity Centre, 2006)

Britain's demographic change

Britain's changing demographics are eye-catching. Pensioners now total 11.5 million, nearly a fifth of the UK population. We have just passed a milestone which means that, for the first time since records began, the number of people of pensionable age (60 for women and 65 for men) exceeds the number of children under 16. This landmark announcement made by the Office of National Statistics in August 2008 sent the media into an immediate flurry, searching for experts to explain what it all meant. Mervyn Kohler, Head of Public Affairs at charity Help the Aged, cogently explained in *The Independent*: 'The days of assuming older people are dependants must now come to an end. These figures clearly show the economic harm that will be caused to UK plc by continuing to exclude older people from the active workforce.'

In the same article, business leaders warned that an increase in life expectancy, coupled with the fact that 12 million Britons have not saved enough for retirement, means there is a need to ensure people work beyond the retirement age. Neil Carberry, Head of Employment Policy at the Confederation of British Industry, said: 'As the baby-boom generation retires we are likely to see significant increases in the ratio of retired people in the workforce. We are going to see many people will choose to work longer.'

The age-balance of Britain's workforce has in fact been changing for some time, as the first batch of baby boomers reach retirement age. In some highly skilled areas such as aerospace and defence, up to 40 per cent of the workforce could be leaving in the next five years in line with international trends, according to *The Economist*, taking a lifetime of expertise with them. Professional body City & Guilds has also predicted that from 2010, the number of young people reaching working age will fall by 60,000 every year.

Further predictions estimate that between 2010 and 2020, the UK will need more than two million new workforce entrants. It is now widely acknowledged that this demand can only be met through a combination of most adults extending their working life and enticing many more to re-enter the labour market. Whilst the scales have already been tipped in the UK with pensioners now outnumbering children, in the next decade it is predicted that there will be more people aged over 40 than under 40.

Advances in medical care and greater awareness of health and diet have made a key impact, so much so that the fastest growing age group in Britain are the over-80s who now number 2.7 million, more than five per cent of the population. In line with a falling mortality rate and increased life expectancy, there has also been a significant drop in fertility rates to 1.73 births per woman, which is below the general population replacement level of 2.1 births per woman.

All of this has resulted in what researchers call a 'deteriorating dependency ratio' where there is a higher percentage of people who are economically inactive yet are supported by a workforce that is both shrinking and ageing. A 'demographic time bomb' of this type points only one way – towards a greater consideration by UK employers of challenges presented in recruiting, engaging and retaining older workers.

A global picture of ageing

Such scenarios are not confined to British shores. Current estimates stand that by 2050 the average age of Europe's population will be 49 and one in three will be retired. So the UK is in very good company with Germany, Italy and Spain when it comes to population ageing. In Asia, Japan's crown as the greyest of them all is challenged by Singapore, which will have a third of its population over 65 by 2050, and South Korea, which today has a particularly low fertility rate of just 1.09 births per woman.

These nations have been described by Stanford Center on Longevity as the 'oldest' countries – the most acute cases in terms of shrinking working-age populations and growing fiscal burdens imposed by so many retirees. At the next level down, we find the 'middle-age' countries facing much the same demographic curve with fertility rates approaching or falling below the replacement rate and slowing workforce growth requiring productivity gains to offset the negative economic consequences. Into this category fall Brazil, Mexico, Australia and China, a nation that will have 400 million citizens over 65 in the next 20 years and whose average age of 25 in 1950 will shoot up to 45 by 2050.

On the bottom rung we find 'young countries' like India, Pakistan, Iraq and Nigeria which still have relatively high fertility rates and rapid growth in working-age populations. However these countries face demographic problems of their own in that their economies must provide paid work for large numbers of young adults, and run the risk of political instability and unrest if they fail to address the 'youth bulge' in their workforce.

Australia follows the age curve

Australia is an interesting example of a 'middle-age' country. It is widely depicted as a young nation but its population growth under 40 has slowed noticeably and by 2010 one in five Australians will be 60 or over, rising to one in four by 2025. Currently there are 5.25 people in the Australian workforce for every person aged 65 and over. By 2050 this will have fallen to just 2.2 people. The pressure is clearly on. Since the 1990s Australia's Federal and State Governments have introduced a number of legislative and policy changes in an attempt to remove the incentive for early retirement amongst Australia's ageing population, and to increase the mature workforce pool.

Many older Australians, especially senior managers, are reported as keen to continue working if they can do so on a more flexible basis. However research has found that such flexible arrangements are usually only offered in lower-paid jobs. The link between older workers and knowledge workers is explicit in Australian labour trends with more than 40 per cent of workers in the higher-skill occupation group of managers and administrators reported as aged 45–64. The big challenge in Australia and elsewhere is to retain these experienced people and prevent knowledge and expertise from draining out of the organisation.

Policy as a panacea

Legislation is one way to stem the age-related brain drain. In the UK, the introduction of the Employment Equality (Age) Regulations (2006) now requires organisations to remove age bias from all aspects of employment including: recruitment, selection, promotion, training and development, redundancy and retirement. In addition, the guidelines laid out in the Disability Discrimination Acts of 1995 and 2004 set out the need for the design of the workplace to consider access for older and disabled people. It is therefore becoming vital that work environments not only address the potential needs of an older workforce as good business management, but also as a requirement that can be enforced by law.

Further UK Government strategy to address the demographic shift has been laid out in the 2005 White Paper *Opportunity Age*. Policy aims to encourage older people to stay in employment for longer as well as supporting employers to use their older workforce more productively. The White Paper proposes that a million more older workers should be engaged in the workforce, that age positive campaigns be used to address negative employer attitudes towards older workers and that new pension rules offer incentives to those who defer drawing their state pension.

Further pension reforms have been laid out in the White Paper *Security in Retirement: Towards a New Pensions System* which attempts to simplify the current pensions system, linking state pensions to average earnings, offering pension credit for time spent caring for children and others, and progressively raising the state pension age from 65 to an age linked to increasing life expectancy.

Such policy proposals tend to be reported unfavourably in the British media as 'work till you drop'. But there is now growing recognition that stock market convulsions, which adversely affect pension fund valuations, are making such reforms even more urgent. It is also clear that many people of retirement age want to continue working – and some organisations in the UK are attempting to meet this need. The Chartered Institute of Personnel Development reports that a wide range of organizations, from Hertfordshire County Council to the supermarket Asda, have removed their mandatory retirement age, whilst the building society Nationwide has increased its retirement age to 75.

The issue of what age we retire has been working its way through the British Courts: the default age of 65 was the subject of a legal challenge at the end of 2007 and the UK Government is set to review the default retirement age by 2011, yet could be superseded by a ruling from the European Court of Justice. But even if the official retirement age in the UK is legally raised, there are problems to be addressed for the ageing workforce. Historically, there have been relatively low rates of workforce participation for those aged between 50 and 65 and recent data suggests that just 10 per cent of women and eight per cent of men are in employment after the normal retirement age.

Such a trend exacerbates the skills shortages that are causing concern to many organisations. The Cranfield School of Management reports that nearly eight out of ten employers experience difficulty in recruiting the right people with the right skills. As the younger proportion of the workforce continues to shrink, motivating and attracting a large pool of experienced workers becomes a commercial priority.

At least people in Britain now appear reconciled to working past the current state pension age, according to data from the English Longitudinal Study of Ageing (ELSA), published in 2008. A third of men aged between 60 and 64 said they expected to carry on working past 65, compared to only a quarter five years before. Women between 55 and 59 expressed similar views: 45 per cent expected to carry on working past the age of 60, compared to only 35 per cent five years previously. Key factors in keeping people in the workplace are levels of education and health. Those with the least qualifications and the lowest levels of fitness and well-being are most likely to be lost to the workforce.

International responses to the problem

These shifts are not unique to the UK but part of a global phenomenon. In 2002, the United Nations unveiled the International Plan on Ageing, which not only recognised the rights of older people to continue to work but also emphasised the wider social benefits of their continued employment. These benefits include not only relieving the burden of state pensions and other welfare payments but also retaining key knowledge and skills within a company or sector – that all-important social capital.

In Germany, there are schemes like those at manufacturing firm MicroTec, to bring young and senior engineers and technicians into the same team, so that older workers can update their technological skills and novices can learn from experienced heads. In China, there are government funds to enable a pool of six million retirees with professional and technical backgrounds to start their own businesses. In India, where there is a currently a retirement age of 58, an online job portal set up by the Dignity Foundation is allowing millions of 'silver surfers' to place their resumés on the web for employers to search.

Meanwhile policymakers everywhere are keeping their fingers crossed that a greater proportion of older people will choose to remain active in the workplace. In those countries that have legislated, seniors are buoyed by age and disability legislation in place to protect their rights and ensure their needs are met. But employers will also have to do their bit, not least in designing their workplaces more effectively to address the inevitable physical effects of ageing in the workforce. As we shall discuss, ageing employees require a watchful approach in terms of physical access, lighting, acoustics, air quality, furniture, ergonomics, spatial planning, material finishes, assistive technology and so on. But then, so do all employees whose expertise, knowledge and productivity are to be valued.

3 Knowledge workers

They're here but we don't know how to make them productive

While the workforce has been ageing rapidly, it has been transforming itself in other ways too, most notably in the approach to and training for work as more jobs have migrated from manual labour and repetitive process tasks to the more flexible and fast-changing knowledge economy. Doctors, lawyers, academics, accountants and scientists were among the first knowledge workers identified as a group around 1960 simultaneously but independently by two American economists, Peter Drucker and Fritz Machlup. But the term 'knowledge worker' can now be routinely applied to most executive and managerial roles within business, industry, professional services and the public sector.

Knowledge work even straddles both manual and white-collar work. Long after his first pronouncements on the subject, Drucker himself drew attention to an important new class of worker he described as 'knowledge technologists': computer technicians, software

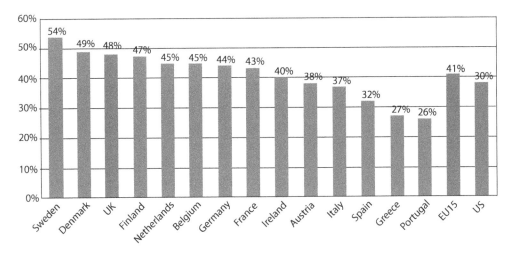

Chart showing percentages of knowledge workers in European workforces
(Eurostat 2007)

designers, analysts in clinical labs, paralegals and so on. This group is swelling the ranks of knowledge workers worldwide by undertaking tasks that require formal education rather than a traditional apprenticeship. Knowledge technologists are tipped by Drucker to become as dominant a force in the twenty-first century workplace as manual labourers were in the twentieth century. Against this background, it is little wonder that working life now increasingly revolves around the emerging idea of a knowledge economy and that statisticians are scurrying to quantify the economic impact of knowledge workers.

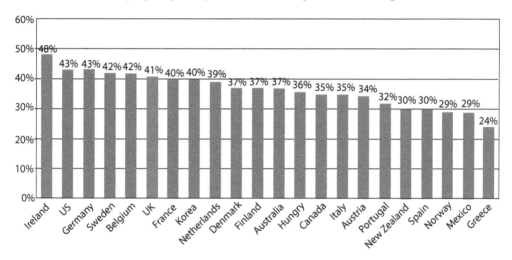

Chart showing percentages of national income derived from knowledge-based industries (OECD 2006)

Quantifying the output

The Organisation for Economic Co-operation and Development (OECD) data indicates that 43 per cent of national income in both the US and Germany is derived from knowledge-based industries. The figure is 41 per cent for the UK and a chart-topping 48 per cent of national income for Ireland. Knowledge-based industries are classified by the OECD as medium to high-tech manufacturing, financial services, business services, telecommunications, education and health services.

According to Eurostat data for the European Commission, 41 per cent of the European workforce is today engaged in the knowledge economy, compared to just 30 per cent in the United States. Within Europe, Sweden (54 per cent) and Denmark (49 per cent) have the most knowledge workers, followed by the UK with 48 per cent. Greece (27 per cent) and Portugal (26 per cent) have the least knowledge workers.

One way to assess the shift in working patterns is to look at research that classifies today's jobs in three areas – transformational, transactional or tacit. Transformational jobs are mainly in taking raw materials and developing them into a finished artefact;

these belong to the manufacturing economy. Transactional work involves routine interactions, often to a script or to a set of rules, and such jobs can be found throughout the service economy. In contrast, tacit jobs involve more complex interactions in which there is more ambiguity; these primarily belong to the knowledge economy.

In a study of tacit interactions, researcher Bradford C Johnson found that 'tacit knowledge workers' are difficult to duplicate and replace. Yet work that involves tacit interactions is growing rapidly: 70 per cent of jobs created in the US since 1998 can be described as based in knowledge work. The study predicts that jobs that draw on the judgement, experience and informed knowledge of workers will 'constitute the core of tomorrow's competitiveness for developed countries'.

Clueless about working conditions

If the future now belongs to knowledge workers, and successful innovation and economic growth depend squarely on their efforts, it is surprising that we should know so little about the conditions in which they are most productive. Forty years after his pioneering research on knowledge work, Peter Drucker felt moved to comment on knowledge-worker productivity: 'We are in the year 2000 roughly where we were in the year 1900 in terms of the productivity of the manual worker.' Productivity of the manual worker increased around 50 times during the twentieth century through process improvements of one kind or another, but can we be so certain that we will nail the requirements for knowledge workers to be as effective? The early signs are not promising.

A key problem is that while manual and process labour has been relatively straightforward to assess and improve, knowledge workers are not nearly so easy to observe, supervise and design for. By its very nature, knowledge work is harder to define, measure and map, as it is mostly invisible, taking place inside the knowledge worker's head. As a result, many knowledge workers find themselves trying to perform within organisational structures, physical environments and technology systems that are outdated and increasingly irrelevant to their needs.

The US management expert Thomas Davenport has commented that knowledge work currently has no twenty-first century equivalent of Frederick Taylor or Henry Ford to drive forward the management and design of the knowledge workplace. Thus, while we may recognise that the traditional management reporting hierarchy or factory-office space plan is not suitable for this new form of work, we struggle to define alternative models and find ways to measure their effectiveness. Quite simply, we just don't know what makes knowledge workers *tick*.

What we know about knowledge workers

We do know some important things about knowledge workers. As well as being more economically significant, they are more mobile than other types of office workers, moving around a lot both within the building and outside the employer's workplace. They enjoy each other's company and tend to cluster in specific geographic areas, whether California's Silicon Valley or London's Shoreditch.

They are specialists, identifying more closely with their profession, knowledge or skill, than with their employer. They are, for instance, far less likely to introduce themselves as 'an IBM man' than as 'a software architect'. They are always alert to a chance to update their knowledge and keep it fresh. They think creatively and experimentally rather than organisationally. They are suspicious of formal hierarchy. As such, they are fast rewriting William Whyte's 1956 classic *The Organisation Man* more along the lines of American academic Richard Florida's best-selling thesis, *The Rise of the Creative Class* (2002).

Knowledge workforces have a higher proportion of women, whose professional qualifications can better negotiate the glass ceiling, and older people, who have spent a long career acquiring their knowledge. In key sectors, knowledge workers are also in scarce supply, making employers nervous about a brain drain or early retirement and more willing to invest in expensive workplaces that will keep them happy and productive. This process has been described, in an article in the *Harvard Business Review*, as 'the battle of capital versus talent'. Management won a resounding victory over the labour unions in the industrial economy of the twentieth century but is finding the wage and other demands of workers in the knowledge economy less easy to resist.

Fad, fashion and faith in redesign

One consequence of this is that companies around the world have begun experimenting heavily with workplace redesign in recent years, in a bid to make their premium knowledge workers more productive. The trouble is, they haven't been learning much from their experiments. According to Thomas Davenport, 'Fad, fashion and faith drive most new work environments for knowledge workers.'

Consider how much workplace redesign has revolved around the introduction of informal and social spaces – streetscapes, coffee bars and the like – devised to encourage greater interaction amongst the knowledge workforce. However many of these alternative spaces remain empty for long periods or are used for conventional meetings. Even when they are occupied more meaningfully, there is little real understanding of how such interactions actually improve performance. People generally lack the confidence to break out from traditional work settings; companies have not prepared the ground in terms of culture change; the new rituals required to make the cutting-edge knowledge workplace succeed have not yet been eased into use.

More than that, the emphasis on collaboration with others as the primary function of knowledge work neglects the need of knowledge workers to concentrate on their own for long periods of time. Nobody would deny the central importance of collaboration within knowledge-intensive organisations. Numerous studies have crystallised its positive impact on business performance; for example, research conducted by Nancy Gofus and colleagues revealed that collaboration has double the impact of a company's strategic direction and five times more impact than market fluctuations.

While the value of tacit knowledge exchange cannot be under-estimated and office environments should be devised to support that exchange, knowledge workers also require peace and quiet to concentrate. Many knowledge creation tasks – writing, editing, analysing, programming and designing, for example – require settings that facilitate solo working without distraction. One study by American researcher Maurice Brill found workers devoting nearly two-thirds of their time (64 per cent) to 'quiet work' – a far cry from the popular media image of the knowledge economy as one big facilitated brainstorm.

Getting the balance right between the needs of collaboration and concentration is just one of the imponderables in designing for knowledge work. Thomas Davenport's research suggests that many companies, unable to clearly identify the needs of their knowledge workforce, have more or less resorted to bribing key knowledge workers with high salaries and, for better or worse, expensively-fabricated settings.

Technology gets in the way

These costly workplaces are often loaded up with the latest technologies – laptops, personal digital assistants, wireless communicators, personal messaging systems, mobile phones and so on – that are perceived as essential for knowledge workers to carry out their work. Indeed technology companies make a habit of targeting this group with 'knowledge worker solutions' – software-driven systems to integrate the many technologies of communication, collaboration and management, offering 'seamless mobility' and other techno-promises.

The trouble is that once these IT solutions have been installed, knowledge workers are often left to fend for themselves without adequate training and support. As a result, technologies are ineffectively deployed and personal information poorly managed. Davenport estimates that a company's most valuable employees may end up spending almost 40 per cent of their working day tied up in knots over IT systems that are not properly integrated to their knowledge tasks. It is one of the maddening ironies of the knowledge economy that people granted high degrees of autonomy and special exemptions from supervisory cultures, precisely because of their expertise and experience, should waste so much time extracting knowledge from the very systems that are meant to support them.

Some companies have introduced coaching and mentoring schemes to combat the mismatch between the promise of new technology and its delivery in knowledge-intensive jobs. Others rely on knowledge workers to work around the problem and find their own way through. There is now a pronounced emphasis on the ability to adapt and change, learn new skills and work longer and faster, even if IT support is minimal. Older workers, who began to acquire their knowledge before computers were on every desk and in every pocket, can be very resentful of this counter-productive approach. Research suggests that workers in industries with high rates of technological change will retire later if there is a positive correlation between technology introduction and on-the-job training.

New ideas are needed

If we take the argument advanced by Davenport and others that the productivity of knowledge workers depends critically on three things – management and organisation, workplace design and information technology – then, in all three areas, it is clear that new ideas are badly needed. Knowledge workers in the early twenty-first century are trying to work around structures, environments and systems that are not fit for their highly specialised, peer-oriented purpose. Office design, the focus of this book, is a particular culprit in terms of a mismatch between mental activities and physical settings in the knowledge economy. But it needs to be integrated with the other two critical factors to have meaning for the people who will hold the key to future organisational success.

4 Burned-out, bottlenecked and bored

What happens when the workplace isn't working

In previous chapters we have talked about the greying of the workforce and the rise of the knowledge economy. So, what happens when highly educated, ageing office workers brush up against organisational, technological and physical barriers in the workplace? A great deal of the productivity gain and innovation potential so prized by today's employers is lost, and companies struggle to find solutions to the problem.

The authors of an influential paper in the *Harvard Business Review* summed it up best when they described millions of mid-career employees – the future and emerging older workforce – as 'burnt-out, bottlenecked and bored'. Researchers Robert Morison, Tamara Erickson and Ken Dychtwald coined a new term – 'middlescence' – to describe the professional frustrations that form when knowledge workers realise they have climbed as far as they can on the career ladder, or are bored stiff with the unchallenging nature of their work.

A key effect of 'middlescence' is that many companies risk losing some of their best and most knowledgeable people. Equally, a draining of energy and enthusiasm for work can result in a loss of business drive and focus. Research suggests that those who are not engaged with their work but stay can be more damaging for an organisation than those who choose to leave. The phenomenon typically affects employees between 35 and 54, a forgotten generation sandwiched between older baby boomers close to retirement and newcomers to the workplace; this group are staring at their own work futures as the older generation and do not like what they see.

Options to revitalise careers

So what is to be done? One strategy is to offer fresh assignments to more senior workers, allowing the employee to move to a different area of the company either departmentally or geographically. Many top firms such as Dow Chemical, Hewlett-Packard and Marriott International have developed career revitalisation programmes that have benefited the employee by allowing new challenges and roles, even if not a straightforward promotion, and benefited the employer by retaining valued members of staff.

Another approach is to offer mentoring schemes, so that the mid-career worker can re-engage by mentoring less experienced colleagues and thus create new social connections and knowledge flows within the workplace. Training budgets can also be redirected from the normal target of younger staff towards older, more experienced people, who are often revitalised by being retrained.

Sabbaticals, more common in higher education than in the corporate sector, can be a judicious way to rejuvenate an employee's flagging morale. Some companies offer workers the opportunity to engage in voluntary work with charities on sabbatical, receiving full pay and benefits whilst directly helping others. The employer's corporate social responsibility agenda is also enhanced.

Expanding leadership development is a further option to revive a bottlenecked knowledge worker. Putting an employee forward for such a programme signals their value and potential, which are so often overlooked in mid-career and especially for the over-50s. Too often such 'fast-track' development is only aimed at the younger members of a company.

Indeed there is no shortage of tricks and tactics to try out. But the piloting of rescue packages to combat 'middlescence' is not just for the frustrated few. Millions of employees are affected because there seems to be a point in the work cycle, usually in mid-career, where older workers, whatever their level of expertise and experience, simply veer off the radar in terms of career training and development. Resistance to investing in older people can sometimes be the direct result of in-built institutional ambivalence towards ageing, sometimes less so. Yet it is important to remember that workers do not become 'older' at a particular age. The physical and psychological effects of ageing are gradual and involve multiple, minor impairments in eyesight, hearing, dexterity, mobility and memory for which thoughtful and inclusive workplace design can readily compensate.

Survivors, jugglers and choosers

According to the UK-based Centre for Research into the Older Workforce (CROW), age discrimination is real and widely experienced by older workers. Much of this discrimination can be seen as unconscious and is based on wider social and cultural perceptions of ageing such as older people being less flexible, not being as capable and not wanting to work as hard. The idea that older people are not worth training as they may be retiring soon is also a widely held prejudice. These negative cultural images of ageing are held collectively by society and are also self-reinforcing in the workplace. So that when older workers bemoan their ageing bodies they feed directly into that wider negative stereotype of age.

The CROW research found that age discrimination is experienced by 7 per cent of the working population. But such discrimination jumps threefold to 21 per cent amongst the over 50s. As such, the experiences of working life may help to determine if an older worker decides to stay in employment or leave. The CROW research suggests that many older workers are faced with one of three choices when making decisions about their later working life. These choices – to survive, juggle or choose – are based on the level of formal qualifications gained throughout life.

'Survivors' are those with few or no qualifications, often working in routine jobs to survive. They have less control over when they work or leave the job market, and are more likely to leave due to ill health. It is estimated that a third of women in the UK work in a 'survival' capacity. In contrast, the majority of women in the workplace are 'jugglers' working in flexible arrangements – often part time. Whilst better qualified than 'survivors', 'jugglers' are also more likely to experience negative changes to their job. The research found that jugglers are the least likely group to continue working at a company after retirement but the most likely to consider taking up voluntary work.

'Choosers' comprise the third category. Unsurprisingly, two-thirds of this group are male. 'Choosers' are highly qualified from managerial or professional careers and they have had a broadly positive experience of working life. They are most likely to continue working after retirement, even though they may have accrued a generous pension, and they are most likely to be found in the knowledge economy where their experience can count most.

More broadly, CROW's body of research points to the willingness to stay in employment being dependent on the extent to which individuals feel in control of their working lives (or perhaps their lives in general). Also the willingness to consider working longer, while high for people in their 50s, declines rapidly with economic inactivity. Therefore strategies to extend working life need to address people before they retire or, at the very least, soon after.

Work Ability in Finland

On this issue we encounter an important concept called Work Ability, which emerged in Finland in the early 1980s. Work Ability is based on the idea of measuring the ability of an individual holistically to sustain a working life. A total of 6,500 workers were studied over a decade to consider the biological effects of ageing on the ability to carry out certain physical work tasks. Work Ability was pioneered by Professor Juhani Ilmarinen, Director of the Department of Physiology in the Finnish Institute of Occupational Health. Concern over the potentially negative economic effects of his country's rapidly ageing population prompted him to study what was causing municipal workers to leave the workforce early and to develop strategies to combat the problems they encountered.

The Finnish study found that, in contrast to those familiar stereotypes about mental feebleness among older people, there are a number of mental characteristics that are strengthened by age. Older workers showed themselves to have more wisdom, sharper wits, the ability to deliberate, reason and comprehend the whole, better verbal command and a better control of life, a higher motivation to learn, a stronger commitment to work and more loyalty to the employer, resulting in less absence from work.

What came out of Ilmarinen's work was the idea that although ageing may decrease the speed of learning, the actual learning process is not impaired and a stronger motivation to learn may compensate for the change in learning speed. Also, while the effects of ageing will inevitably make all of us physically weaker, we can become mentally stronger. Therefore working life should be arranged so that work becomes progressively less physically demanding and more mentally so.

A Work Ability Index was devised combining a number of individual and wider social factors. These include an individual's health and functional capacities, education and competence, values, attitudes and motivation – all considered in relation to the wider physical and mental work demands, the working community, management and the environment in which the work takes place. Low scores on the Work Ability Index were interpreted as a predictor of early retirement unless interventions were introduced.

The Work Ability concept has attracted widespread international interest as other nations follow Finland on the age curve. Significantly, it has helped to reframe the debate around older workers. Often there is an overwhelming instinct to blame the individual when productivity drops rather than considering the wider factors in which the older employee works. Yet apportioning blame is no longer socially acceptable or good for business. The need to keep older knowledge workers economically active for longer demands a different approach. Interventions to achieve this can range from new methods to train older staff in new technology to physical design changes that make the work environment more age-friendly, on which we have much more to say later.

Capturing design requirements

To get a better idea of what interventions might be most favourable to older knowledge workers, architectural researchers Harriet Harriss and Suzi Winstanley of the Royal College of Art, London, published a study in 2005 called *Capture It*, supported by US furniture company Steelcase and other partners. What they discovered through design-based ethnographic research with individuals and organisations, including Kita-Kyushu, a Japanese engineering consulting firm comprised entirely of post-retirees, was revealing.

Older workers at the Kita-Kyushu company in Japan (RCA, 2005)

Older workers wanted more choice and control over when they work, not only during the working day but over the working week. Such flexibility would be crucial for those managing other aspects of life such as child-minding grandchildren or caring for elderly parents. Similar to the Finnish research, *Capture It* also found that older workers were curious and committed to learning, but also that many take what they learn in a professional capacity and use it to develop their personal interests.

The study identified a need for space and time for reflection and contemplation, in recognition of the fact that many older workers are flexible or part-time workers balancing a mixed portfolio and working, in Peter Drucker's term, 'at arm's length' from the organisation. These arrangements are inherently stressful to manage. Reflective spaces would require a feeling of being closer to nature. In this context, softer, more tactile surfaces in natural materials would replace harsh grey, steel and glass – the brusque masculinity of the corporate environment.

Older workers both wanted access to new technology and separation from its ubiquitous presence, as their lives demanded. Many would like technology training more tailored to their age and experience. They also wanted visual triggers in the work environment to help jog their memory. Finally, the Capture *It* study revealed that older workers do not want to be singled out, cocooned or ghettoised with their peers. They want to connect with colleagues across the generations and, through mentoring schemes, offer valuable wisdom and guidance.

Design scenario from Capture It study
by Harriet Harris and Suzi Winstanley
(RCA, 2005)

Devising a design agenda

Through this and other studies, a design agenda of sorts begins to emerge for older workers in the knowledge economy, whether they are bored and bottlenecked in mid-career or burnt out and contemplating quitting the workforce altogether. Already, mindful of the impact of demographic change, the manufacturing economy has been gearing up for the ageing workforce. According to a special report in *The Economist*, Illinois-based industrial equipment manufacturer Deere & Company is using a mix of flexible working, telecommuting and ergonomic factory design to extend working lives. Around 35 per cent of its 46,000 employees are over 50, with a number over 70. Deere is on a mission to make the job less tiring.

In the same vein, Toyota has adapted its standard workstation to the needs of older workers and BMW has built a factory at Leipzig, Germany expressly to employ people over 45. Both of these examples illustrate measures to counter a lack of skilled labour in the automotive industry. It is time for knowledge-based organisations to follow suit in adapting the workplace to accommodate a wider range of age and ability. But, as we have already pointed out, making the right moves to boost knowledge worker productivity is a much more complex affair. In the following chapters we examine what has been happening in office design to plan for change.

5 An unholy alliance

A conspiracy of management process and modern design

Why are we struggling to find answers to the office environment needs of a changing workforce in the early years of the twenty-first century? Why are so many office buildings too noisy, complex, tiring and distracting for older workers? Why are so many work settings too rigid and inflexible to accommodate the more fluid knowledge interactions of contemporary business practice? At least some of the answers can be found in the way modern office design established itself as the answer to the need for management efficiency in the twentieth century.

As organisations sought to maintain the whiphand over employees, transferring legacies of control from the factory to the office space, the industrial and engineering metaphors of so much management theory was mirrored by the functionalist design dogma of modernist offices with their hard edges and 'efficient' rectilinear forms.

There was a moment in time when architects, space planners and interior designers – the professional consultants of three-dimensional form, to whom organisations turn for advice on how to accommodate and support the processes of work – subscribed en masse to the universal ideologies of the Modern Movement. The office was given pride of place by designers as a testbed for modernist ideas – a place of rational production and administration, like the factory, whose aesthetic should almost entirely be determined by the considerations of management efficiency. No comfort zones for ageing bodies or subtle minds here.

Over the course of the twentieth century, the powerful visual image of rigid organisational control became the norm from which many employers now have trouble departing. With the benefit of hindsight, we can see that there was, in the early years of the last century, both a collision and a collusion between the needs of fast-growing organisations to control their functions and the emerging creed of modernist and machine-age design, as the first modern offices grew rapidly out the bureaucratisation of industry.

Work ethic and aesthetic

The work aesthetic was closely modelled on the work ethic. Designers became as fascinated by the rational and geometric image of the machine – by turbines, automobiles and aeroplanes – as their nineteenth-century predecessors had been inspired by irrational and organic forces of nature, by waterfalls, petals and caves. Modernist designers turned functionalism of the kind that bends people to the will of the system into an entire visual design movement surprisingly resistant to change.

It was, of course, an essentially negative combination. Pseudo-scientific analysis of management processes and modernist design ideology aided and abetted each other in their neglect of human factors, group psychology, changing needs, and the requirement to build elaborate networks of social relationships within organisations in order for them to be successful.

Conspiracy theorists lead us directly to one man – Frederick Taylor (1856–1915), the proponent of scientific management, and the progenitor of work study and of a whole school of twentieth-century organisational analyses. Taylor was an American engineer who adapted the time-and-motion studies of the factory floor to the emerging office environment. He understood better than anyone before him how the standardisation of work tools and conditions could improve productivity.

Determined to develop what he called 'superior methods and machines', Taylor took a giant spanner to the workplace and tightened all the nuts. By 1911, the year 'efficiency fever' peaked in the United States, Taylor had even decreed that conversation should be banned in the office on the grounds that it interrupted work. Critics have pointed out that Taylor has been a more powerful and durable influence on the look and style of the workplace than even the Bauhaus, the German design school of the 1920s which became the fountainhead of functionalist design. Taylor's ideas were held up in US business schools such as Harvard and Wharton, and even studied closely in China and the USSR.

Giant pieces of engineering

In the post-1945 years, a host of Taylorist followers began to treat organisations, in the management writer Charles Handy's phrase, as 'giant pieces of engineering'. The notion of careful allocation of tasks, responsibilities and spans of control, and particularly the emphasis on process analysis and control, fed through into the quality movement led by men like Deming and Juran, and could seen in such practices as Business Process Re-Engineering and Benchmarking, both of which are now viewed with some suspicion by contemporary organisational experts wrestling with a complex business dynamic.

Architects and designers followed a similar line to the system fanatics in management, inspired by the Bauhaus architect Mies van der Rohe's dictum that the office is a machine for working in. When Bauhaus tutors such as Walter Gropius, Mies van der Rohe, Marcel Breuer and Laszlo Moholy-Nagy fled from the Nazis in the 1930s to spread their gospel in Britain and America, the fundamentals of the Bauhaus curriculum became the basis for decades of architectural and design training in the US and UK. Offices were destined to look and feel like 'machines'.

By the time Le Corbusier wrote enthusiastically in *Towards A New Architecture* (1946) about 'admirable office furniture' as one of the most significant new objects of modern life and Mies van der Rohe sold the ideals of the Bauhaus to American big business with his 1958 glass-block Seagram Building, a landmark in functionalist corporate environments, the Modern Movement signature design had become the perfect encapsulation of corporate control.

This was in itself a curious state of affairs. The satirical writer Tom Wolfe has mocked, in *From Bauhaus to Our House* (1979), the historical irony by which cheap geometric worker housing designed for the crisis-torn Weimar Republic by morally-driven Bauhaus academics became the unchallenged architectural blueprint for 'the very Babylon of capitalism' – America in the 1950s and 1960s. But the power of giving the process of scientific management a recognisable and easily replicated visual language should not be underestimated.

The pseudo-scientific language Frederick Taylor used to define organisational problems and the largely mechanistic techniques he adopted to try and solve them undeniably enjoyed some valid intellectual basis – just as similar metaphors and analytical techniques guided design disciplines in the mid-twentieth century. There are certainly process problems within organisations that may be amenable to detailed project analysis and process re-engineering – and fundamental engineering principles must inevitably underlie the aesthetic content of good three-dimensional design.

But one has only to observe the demotivation that lies beneath many apparently well-designed factories and offices, or the social disasters behind many grandiose 1960s housing schemes or recast cityscapes, to understand that process-driven pseudo-science did not serve us well in terms of creating sympathetic living and working environments in the twentieth century. Indeed there is a widespread belief that we need to do much better now.

Making pseudo-science visible

Today it is accepted that design is about meeting people's needs at a particular social, economic and cultural junction, not about adhering to a process-based credo. But the passive design emulators of the pioneer modernists increasingly failed to see it like that. In their essentially aesthetic approach, they made pseudo-scientific management process respectable simply because they made it so visible.

So how can we mend the fractures in our workplace culture that the alliance of management efficiency and modern design throughout the twentieth century has bequeathed us? To institute a more holistic and user-centred approach to office design requires a clear analysis of recent design experiments in the field.

6   Collaborative working

Open-plan experiments without conclusive results

Faced with a changing workforce and eager to address the deficiencies of the past, the architects, developers and specifiers who shape the contemporary landscape of workplace design have not been short of new ideas over the past decade. Office buildings and environments around the world have been the focus of intense design investment mainly pointing in one general direction – towards the primacy of collaboration and work as a social activity. This in itself has been no bad thing, tilting the balance from an overriding focus on management efficiency towards the human factors of individual performance. One can only applaud consistent attempts to achieve a tighter fit between corporate culture and work environment.

However, while there have been new concepts aplenty, real progress has been patchy and a standard body of evidence on best design practice in relation to organisational productivity has stubbornly refused to take shape. When Dr Frank Duffy of architects DEGW, one of the world's leading workplace design theorists, introduced a major new British study on the subject in 2005, called *The Impact of Office Design on Business Performance*, he memorably observed: 'The collective failure to understand the relationship between the working environment and business purpose puts us in the position of early nineteenth century physicians, with their limited and erroneous notions about the transmission of disease before the science of epidemiology had been firmly established.'

The study that Duffy fronted for the BCO (British Council for Offices) and CABE (Commission for Architecture and the Built Environment) emphasised how the construction and running costs of office buildings are dwarfed by the salaries and other benefits paid to employees: over the 25-year life of a typical office scheme, for example, 85 per cent of all costs goes on paying the occupants. In this context, one can only wonder why more has not been done to tailor the environment more closely to individual user needs. At least the needs of knowledge workers have received plenty of attention. Older workers have been largely ignored by workplace design researchers in favour of what economists term the 'family formation workforce' in the 20–45 age group, which partly explains the low levels of workforce participation among older age groups.

Satisfaction enhances productivity

The BCO/CABE report identified the issue of staff satisfaction as a primary factor in enhancing knowledge worker productivity – it produced research showing that the workplace is responsible for 24 per cent of total job satisfaction and this can affect staff performance by 5 per cent for individuals and 11 per cent for teams. Its message was simple: poor workplace design reduces business performance and raises stress levels among employees. The study reinforced what was already widely known and acknowledged by its authors – British business has a lot of ground to make up in office design to improve levels of satisfaction and productivity.

In 1999, a Ph.D study of 3,000 office employees by Dr Nomana Anjum at the University of Dundee discovered that about one-fifth of UK workplaces failed to provide an adequate work environment and that staff in a quarter of UK offices had serious complaints about such environmental factors as layout, furniture, temperature, noise control and so on. Four years later, in 2003, the magazine *Management Today* with ICM Research canvassed 600 senior managers in the UK and discovered that 45 per cent would consider changing companies – even if the role, salary and benefits in the new job were identical – in return for a better work environment. Managers understood clearly the benefits of a well-designed workplace in terms of raising morale, retaining staff, reinforcing brand identity and driving up productivity.

Right at the top of the executive wishlist was the provision of relaxation/thinking spaces, a reflection of how difficult it could be to do simple things like book a meeting room in most organisations. However nearly a third of those surveyed said they'd be ashamed to bring clients or contacts into their own workplace. This was despite six out of ten managers saying that the design of their office had been reviewed within the past 12 months.

Clearly a large volume of frenetic workplace redesign has not got employers very far in improving productivity – a state of affairs not confined to Britain. In 2002, Thomas Davenport and two colleagues at the management consulting firm Accenture, Bob Thomas and Sue Cantrell, interviewed 41 US companies with initiatives underway to improve the performance of high-end knowledge workers vital to organisational success. 'We found an astounding lack of knowledge about what actually improves performance,' remarked the researchers. All the expensive experiments with indoor boulevards, talk plazas and cappuccino bars – all designed to encourage a social life at work – were not actually telling companies very much about how to support their most valuable employees.

Segmentation and choice

Based on their research, Davenport, Thomas and Cantrell wrote a paper for the *MIT Sloan Management Review* (2002) in which they proposed differentiating work environments for knowledge workers according to two variables: first, the level of segmentation of the work setting based on status, tasks and so on; and second, the level of choice given to the individual. This approach avoided treating all knowledge workers as one homogenous mass and opened up the opportunity, in theory at least, for some differentiation based on age and physical ability.

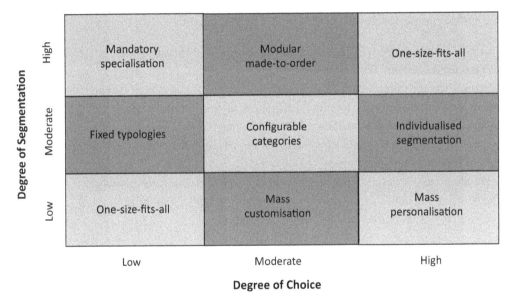

Chart showing knowledge worker framework from Davenport, Thomas and Cantrell (MIT Sloan Management Review, 2007)

Their framework created a range of possibilities – from 'one-size-fits-all' environments, offering a low level of both segmentation and choice, to 'one-size-fits-one' environments offering a high level of segmentation and choice to the individual. In between there were many options: for example, an organisation seeking to grant its employees a high degree of choice, but whose workers' needs vary little and require no segmentation, might adopt a 'mass personalisation' approach to boost employee satisfaction, allowing them to bring in their own artefacts or pets. At the other end of the spectrum, companies with a diverse and unpredictable work setting needs might adopt a high-segmentation approach, with specialist labs or project rooms for example, while offering employees little individual choice. This mandatory specialisation would enable employers to manage unpredictability more effectively.

The rise of open plan

But despite the range of options tantalisingly put forward by this framework, the truth is that most organisations have followed the path of least resistance and adopted a low-segmentation, low-choice approach whatever the needs of their knowledge workers. This is because a simple one-size-fits-all design solution has been at hand. As organisations facing tougher competition in a globalised, knowledge-led economy have sought to simultaneously reduce costs and improve teamwork and communication, uniform open-plan working has presented itself as the most viable option.

In the British workplace in particular, it has been hard to argue against the wisdom of going open-plan in recent years. Not only is open-plan space usually more cost efficient in comparison with cellular accommodation but it also brings the potential benefits of more collaborative ways of working. Mindful of these factors, a wide variety of different organisations have sent their workforces scurrying into open-plan schemes in recent years. From city workers to civil servants, from research scientists to real-estate experts, a whole new generation of people in the knowledge economy are experiencing the joys and frustrations of a world without walls.

Dissenters who argue that open plan by itself is not the total solution to the demands of knowledge work, find it hard to make their voice heard above the clamour to proclaim collaboration above all else as the key to making innovation happen. Within more progressive organisations, the contemporary office has thus become synonymous with one big brainstorm, as Davenport and colleagues discovered.

Successive reviews of new workplace design have illustrated the supremacy of open-plan spaces over other arrangements, even though the reality of these schemes for many older knowledge workers is that they are noisy, distracting, tiring and generally unhelpful to getting the real work done.

The situation is made worse by desk-sharing schemes such as hot-desking and hoteling, which save costs but are generally unpopular, and the brand-aware tendency in many office design projects towards total transparency. Everyone is out in the open, on parade and with nowhere to hide from the collaborative hum of working life. There is no space for quiet or privacy or reflection, whether at the desk or in a social space. Breakout areas, originally conceived as offering a break from work, are now connected with wireless technology for greater working efficiency. There is often simply no escape.

Problems with open plan

Of course nobody would want to go back to the bad old days of long corridors, private rooms and communication by formal memo. Open plan has helped to revolutionise work practices in many organisations. But one is forced to ask whether the pendulum has perhaps swung too far in favour of collaboration at the expense of being able to concentrate for extended periods of time. Some dispatches from the office frontline suggest that all is not always well with open plan working.

Consider the radical workplace experiment that life sciences pioneer Monsanto instituted at its St Louis headquarters in the late 1990s: an exemplary pilot environment for the company's senior executives which abolished private offices in favour of a more open scheme incorporating the metaphors of 'porch', 'parlour' and public 'meadow'. The idea was to encourage informal and unexpected interaction between the company's decision-makers but, over time, Monsanto's senior people overturned the policy and erected their own private spaces.

Then there is the case of Sussex University's £10 million open-plan Freeman Centre. Opened in the UK in 2003, this was designed – again in exemplary fashion and involving user consultation – to be a model of collaborative research but prompted bitter infighting among academics. Documents leaked to the press revealed a collapse of collegiality at one of the world's leading centres for science policy research as researchers squabbled over noisy telephone conversations and confidential papers getting into the wrong hands. In this acrimonious dispute, the problems of finding the right space for knowledge work in its purest form appeared to be crystallised. As Roger Kline of the University and College Union told *The Times Higher*: 'Aside from the obvious problems for studious academics needing private space for research, there is a growing amount of health and safety research that shows open-plan offices can be stressful environments.'

Under the heading 'Open plan or open warfare?' an editorial in *The Times Higher* observed that professionals in many fields, including heads of industry and senior civil servants, managed perfectly well to concentrate on tricky jobs while working amid hubbub. However there was a rider: 'Objectors are right to say that closeness does not guarantee collaboration or cohesion. The way to get people to work together is through properly planned methods such as seminars and joint meetings, not enforced proximity.'

The editorial concluded by saying that as open-plan working had been adopted by most areas of the economy, so it was bound to be part of the solution at universities. But in that phrase 'part of the solution' there opens up a horizon for a more mixed and sophisticated approach to getting workspace right for people on whose ability to think we will increasingly depend.

7 Flexible working

A networked approach for a volatile economy

Parallel with the shift towards collaborative and open working, there has also been a focus on flexibility in office design in recent years. This has manifested itself in many ways – from building projects with column-free internal spaces and floor plates that can be successfully subdivided into discrete units for multiple occupancy of office buildings as occupier demand ebbs and flows, to space-planning schemes with drop-in zones and hot desks that reflect the more mobile and unpredictable patterns of knowledge work in the digital age. Much work has simply moved outside the employer's office, into the home and onto the sites of clients and customers.

New, more flexible ways of working have had a devastating effect on traditional occupancy rates in offices. Many companies have discovered that workstation utilisation in organisations where everyone has their own desk can regularly be lower than 50 per cent and sometimes as low as 20 per cent. Renting, heating and lighting acres of unoccupied workspace is a major headache for financial and property directors who are searching for design solutions that recognise that knowledge workers are more likely to be on the move than previous generations of sedentary office clerks.

The networked office

DEGW's Frank Duffy has published widely on what he describes as a third wave of office design, in specific response to the fluctuations of the knowledge economy. He calls this wave the 'networked office'. The first wave, according to Duffy, was the 'Taylorist office' of the early twentieth century (after Frederick Taylor, as previously discussed). This was an engine of US economic growth and a reflection of the hierarchical management efficiency required to support the manufacturing economy. The second wave was the post-1945 emergence of a 'social democratic office' in Europe. This was a light and bright post-war reaction to the darkness of Fascism, which reflected the rising power of the white-collar unions, considered the well-being and identity of workers, as well as efficiency, and prefigured the budding of the service economy.

While key elements of both the Taylorist and social democratic office endure to this day, the 'networked office' is different. It is led neither by developers as in the Taylorist era, nor by owner-occupiers implementing social democratic principles, but by service providers offering office space for the time you need it. Occupiers of networked offices operate via shorter leases and pay-as-you-go arrangements across a mix of physical and virtual space. In this context, flexibility and connectivity are essential. Whereas in the past organisations tended to provide location-specific settings for work, which they owned or held on a long lease, they now think in terms of a more flexible network of locations, with each office a node in the network.

Many different types of organisation have begun to adopt networked office strategies – from the BBC with its media villages in White City and Salford Docks to the global management consulting firm Accenture. The networked office model provides greater flexibility than the social democratic model and uses new technology to make more efficient, just-in-time use of space than even Frederick Taylor could have imagined, sometimes on a shared, alliance or hired basis.

The powerful branding statements that began in the late 1990s with brand-owner-occupiers such as Reebok, Sony, Quiksilver, Toyota, Bloomberg and others using their work interiors to project brand values has continued into the networked era. However the 'brandscapes' in networked offices are more temporary and transient – more like stage sets – in keeping with the constant morphing of contemporary business practice. As Frank Duffy has observed: 'The new economy is characterised by a shift from value residing in tangible assets (bricks and mortar) to intangible assets such as intellectual property and knowledge.' Office accommodation has simply followed suit. But where does that restless, non-territorial approach leave the demands of knowledge workers for collaborative space, or older workers for comfort?

Working across locations

The first international survey of new office design schemes dedicated to the requirements of knowledge workers, published in 2006 by UK researchers Myerson and Ross, studied 43 cases from around the world and mapped how mobile knowledge workers are no longer confined to the corporate campus, but work across a continuum of different locations: employer's office, settings for professional associations and networks, the city and home. Four key trends emerged for the study.

First, the researchers observed that the corporate headquarters – the traditional site for companies – is being remodelled along the lines of a university campus to encourage more knowledge sharing and collaboration. This trend was named the 'Academy'. Academy-style offices tend to emphasise breakout space, brainstorm rooms and chill-out zones; their atria and courtyards are derived from the historic university quadrangle. Work in these buildings is becoming a more social activity, along the lines that Davenport and his team tried to measure and understand.

Second, the case studies showed that many knowledge workers prefer to spend their working day off-site in the company of their professional peers rather than with fellow employees, with whom they have little in common. They flock to the meeting rooms and exchange spaces of business centres, professional associations, media villages or scientific institutions. This trend was called the 'Guild' because guild-like workspaces are in a sense replicating the medieval craft guild, which clustered those sharing a particular skill or specialism in one place. Many employers are now encouraging this professional clustering to reduce pressure on their own space.

Third, many organisations in an age of open innovation are keen for staff to get away from the sealed campus and closer to their clients and customers. That means having a more permeable relationship with the city and the marketplace – either by enabling public thoroughfares through office buildings, providing public facilities such as art galleries or creating workspace within mixed use developments, retail schemes or landmark civic buildings. This trend was named the 'Agora', after the Greek word for the open trading space in the heart of ancient Athens. As well as shopping destinations and public buildings, many former industrial sites such as warehouses and factories are being remodelled into Agora-style workplaces due to their prominent public location.

Finally, while home-working is not a complete alternative in itself, the home is a valuable supplementary space for knowledge workers. Telltale signs include a rise in live-work units in urban areas as well as a more flexible approach to living space to accommodate work and a more domestic style to workspace to accommodate a long-hours culture. The researchers called this trend the 'Lodge' as the separate spheres of living and working are blurred in many new developments.

What all these trends add up to is a picture of major change in office property, with companies adopting a mix of spaces to meet the needs of knowledge workers as part of a flexible or networked approach. In many cases, provision of workspace is becoming more imaginatively intertwined with retail, industrial, residential and mixed-use property.

Do novelties work?

Relocation to new and different sites by knowledge-intensive organisations has gone hand-in-hand with a fresh and novelty-laden approach to office interiors. But while knowledge workers have had every conceivable novelty thrust in their direction in the corporate workplace, there is very little hard evidence to suggest that elaborate metaphors (internal parks with artificial grass, bandstands, meadows, town squares, libraries, aquaria and so on) or playful gadgets (swings, hammocks, beanbags, jukeboxes, ping pong tables, football machines) make a quantifiable difference to productivity.

Thomas Davenport has declared: 'Knowledge workers don't care about facilities gewgaws' – even though there is plenty of anecdotal evidence to suggest that such additions can create a fun environment that is more engaging for staff. Here a generational factor kicks in: some novelties are very age-specific. Not all over-50s, for example, want to play on the Nintendo or watch MTV at work every day.

What has not been examined or piloted in any detail is the general office environment for when knowledge workers age. Despite the overwhelming predictability of demographic trends, older workers have received scant mainstream design attention outside the special needs lobby. There are reasons for this neglect, as we shall go on to discuss in the following chapter.

8   The nature of the challenge

Making the workplace more inclusive of changing needs

Both collaborative and flexible work styles – the two dominant trends of the past decade – contain a range of inherent barriers for older knowledge workers. There is the noise and disruption of open plan. There are the stresses and strains of mobile working and 'arm's length' engagement with the organisation. So why has office design failed to really consider the needs of an ageing workforce? Some employees over 50 clearly do not want to attract attention by making individual demands at work, for fear of alerting age-discriminatory bosses or colleagues to their prolonged presence. But, more broadly than that, it has been difficult to categorise older people as economically important within modern working culture. The ageing process has been associated with deficit, decline and incompetence, all of which argue against paid employment.

Inclusive design movement

Over the past 30 years, a powerful international movement has successfully aligned industrial design, architecture and social activism to campaign for better homes, transport and public access for older and disabled people. This has been given different names – inclusive design in the UK and Europe, design for all in Scandinavia, universal design in the US and Japan. However a common feature has been to define older people as having consumer and civil rights – they have not been positioned as active economic contributors, other than in exercising their rights as purchasers. As a result, there has been relatively little debate about their workplace needs.

The first frontiers to be pushed back by the inclusive design movement have necessarily been domestic and public ones, to make homes and access to the built environment more age-friendly so that there is more independence and choice for older and disabled people. Access to the workplace has been less of a priority, although that is changing now given the state of government finances around the world and the rising cost of social welfare for the ageing population.

When, in 2000, the UK Government advanced a formal definition of inclusive design as a process whereby 'designers ensure that their products and services address the needs of the widest possible audience', it was talking mainly about such things as easy-to-open packaging, safer bathrooms and low-access buses – office design was not on the radar. But by the time a British Standard for managing inclusive design was written in 2005, advocating that products and services should be 'usable by people with the widest range of abilities within the widest range of situations without the need for special adaptation or design', extended working lives had come into the picture.

Reacting against one-size-fits-all

Historically, in the developed world, inclusive design can be seen as a response to the context of design for mass production in the second half of the twentieth century. In that era of rapid economic and bureaucratic expansion, professional designers working on product development treated people as 'universal types'. An important text of the period for designers, *The Measure of Man* (1960) by the American industrial designer Henry Dreyfuss, established the study of anthropometrics – the dimensions of 'human scale', including arm and leg reach – as an essential tool for designers. This work by Dreyfuss, who measured hundreds of men, women and children and calculated mean averages, supported the mass production doctrine 'one-size-fits-all'. Those on the margins of society who did not conform in terms of height, weight, mental capacity or physical strength were forced to fit in with assumptions about what is 'average' or 'normal'.

The impact of *The Measure of Man* was profound: its thinking influenced the design of everything from packaging, homes and public buildings to furniture, appliances and transport. Its doctrine was especially influential in the low segmentation-low choice workplace as a template for management efficiency. Older and disabled people who clearly did not fit these carefully calculated norms were treated as special cases or groups falling outside the mainstream and requiring special design solutions. A whole activity arose around the development of special needs design for these special needs. This area of design grew outside the mainstream design discourse about lifestyle, aesthetics, needs and desires.

With its limited markets and small production runs, special needs design was blighted by an approach more akin to hospital aids and appliances than consumer-based design. Many products and environments for older and disabled people stigmatised their users through ugly and inappropriate design. Gradually, however, there was a powerful reaction against this stigmatising approach in the design profession. It began slowly at first – catalysed by a few charismatic individuals – but built up into a vocal movement to integrate more people into the mainstream of everyday life through a more inclusive approach to the design of products and services based on desire and aspiration and not just special need.

An onus on the employer

Significantly, there was also a shift towards a more enlightened view that people are not disabled by their own impairments, irrespective of the shortcomings of design, but included or excluded by the quality of design, irrespective of their capabilities. With the emergence of inclusive design came a transfer of responsibility from the user of design to the design process itself. If designers – and the organisations that commissioned them – didn't accept responsibility for what happens when people tried to use their designs, then the net outcome would be exclusion by design.

In the context of the workplace, this was destined to become a highly significant shift. It meant that older workers, like older consumers, would no longer feel it was their own fault when products and environments excluded them or did not meet their needs. Responsibility shifted to the employer who was encouraged, in no small part by age and disability discrimination, to do as much as possible to avoid excluding any workers from the office environment.

Physical requirements

For an ageing workforce, there are a number of physical requirements that form a baseline for thinking about a more inclusively designed workplace. Take eyesight, for example. Adult vision declines with age in a number of ways. The eye of a 20-year-old can admit up to three times more light than someone of 65. Changes occur in visual acuity, depth perception and peripheral vision. As a result many older workers may find glare from windows on a computer terminal affecting their sight.

Research also suggests that older workers often cannot read as well as they once did from certain distances and with lower levels of illumination. Personal preferences regarding lighting conditions become more important with age and people adapt less well to poor lighting. However where good quality lighting is provided, vision changes generally have little impact on most older knowledge workers.

Hearing generally begins to decline from the mid-40s onwards. Older people may struggle to hear well at higher frequencies, for example, being unable to listen to a specific voice or sound in a noisy environment. Workers may find it increasingly difficult to filter a particular voice from background noise. The means to address hearing difficulties will vary depending on the particular office setting, but consideration should always be given to how sound transmission can be controlled.

Consideration should also be given to physical ergonomics as signs of ageing and the beginning of loss of functional ability emerge between 40 and 50. This includes a loss of muscular strength, which on average is reduced by 15–20 per cent between the ages of 20 to 60. Ageing causes some loss of range of joint movement and flexibility. Highly repetitive motions can cause physical problems at any age, but as we age we are likely to become more vulnerable to physical wear and tear. In general, ageing may make it harder to maintain good posture and balance and therefore increase the risk of accidents.

Changes in mental capacity also occur with age. Vocabulary and verbal ability remain constant or improve, but some mental processes decline. Speed of thinking, selective attention and information processing tend to be reduced. In addition, spatial skills generally decline. Research has demonstrated that older people are less efficient at navigating three-dimensional environments and need more time and guidance in finding their way. However cognitive problems appear to have a much lower impact on older knowledge workers, who will tend to compensate for any reduction in cognitive functions by drawing on their experience. Similarly, people who have had a lot of education or training over their lifetime are generally able to learn new skills with relative ease.

How to sustain well-being

With an ageing workforce, it is important to consider how the office environment can help to sustain the health and well-being of staff. This encompasses not only the physical dimension of the workplace but also the social aspects of health. In relation to this, dignity and respect are often as important to well-being and productivity as physical ergonomics. This effectively means that all facilities within the workplace should be designed with older workers in mind, irrespective of who uses them. The drive for greater levels of physical and mental well-being is one of the most persuasive factors in promoting an inclusive design approach. Better office design that meets the needs of older workers is very often better design that meets the needs of everyone. As the gerontologist Bernard Isaacs once remarked: 'Design for the young and you exclude the old. Design for the old and you include everyone.' Being aware of the context for inclusive design is therefore very important.

Why user context matters

Although his influential book *The Measure of Man* eventually became a touch-point against which the inclusive design movement rallied, there is a true story told about Henry Dreyfuss that demonstrates his early acknowledgement of user needs and the importance of human factors in design. As a young man in the early 1930s, Dreyfuss was sent from New York to Iowa to discover why a brand new, beautifully decorated RKO movie palace was not drawing the punters, while the local, unventilated fleapit down the road was full to the rafters every night.

Dreyfuss was mystified. He lowered the prices, ran triple features and gave away free food from the cafeteria but still nobody would come. For three days he stood outside the movie house watching the reactions of people wandering by. Then he removed the expensive deep-pile scarlet carpet from the lobby and replaced it with a simple rubber mat. Immediately, like a miracle, the RKO movie palace was full. The problem, as Dreyfuss rightly identified, was that the good Iowa farming folk didn't wasn't to mess up that gorgeous carpet with their muddy boots.

The moral of the story is clear. The RKO movie palace was sumptuously designed with no expense spared. But it just wasn't right for its context. It was inappropriate to its users. More than 70 years later the same holds true for today's offices. The materials, space-plans, equipment and environmental controls that make up the complex picture of workplace design need to be tuned to the needs of changing workforce. The environment must match what the people within the organisation are trying to achieve.

In this first section of the book, we have spent time reviewing the changing contexts in which both knowledge workers and older employees operate. In the following sections, we go on to use the results of our own global research project, *Welcoming Workplace*, to discuss ways to rethink the culture and redesign the environment in the light of these developments, so that the challenge of a changing workforce can be successfully met.

Part Two
Rethinking the culture

'I speak to older colleagues and we agree, we are no longer on the fast track to anywhere'

Senior employee, pharmaceuticals industry, London

9 Towards a welcoming workplace

Designing research to give older workers a voice

Only a very few employers will be immune to the sweeping changes identified and discussed in the first section of this book. Most organisations, in part or whole, will at some stage face the challenge of redesigning their workplaces to enable growing numbers of older people to participate in the twenty-first century knowledge economy. But while it is one thing to broadly recognise the realities brought on by a shifting workscape, it is quite another to make the right moves to coherently and decisively address the needs of a changing workforce.

Studying the context only takes you so far; researching the people who populate your workforce, making use of new design-based techniques to really get under the skin of their working lives, takes you a whole lot further – enabling you to rethink the culture of your organisation. This is what the second section of this book is all about: we want to tell you about a study we conducted at the Royal College of Art, London, which set out to assess the workplace needs of older knowledge workers and the implications for the planning and design of office environments. There are some important pointers to culture change not only in what we discovered from the participants but also in how we conducted the research.

As we have already discussed, this demographic group is largely neglected within the workforce despite their growing importance to economic value creation. They are not vocal in making specialised demands, they rarely draw attention to themselves, and, as a result, they have been left alone in the main to cope as well as they can in environments designed for a standard 'common-denominator' worker. Relatively little attention has been paid to office design that might better support the productivity, health and well-being of older knowledge workers, despite the weight of evidence pointing to the growth of this workforce segment in terms of size and significance.

Our study, entitled *Welcoming Workplace*, aimed to enrich understanding of what such workers need to carry out their daily work successfully, how they interact with their work environment and what aspects of contemporary office design and technology support them in doing their work. A central question for us was what makes the work environment more inclusive. Key corporate decision-makers in such areas as human resources, occupational health, real estate and facilities require answers to such issues. Our study was also intended to inform designers and architects who are developing office space, systems, tools and furniture, to more closely match the needs of ageing workers.

A multidisciplinary approach

To achieve our aims, we assembled a multidisciplinary research team representing the disciplines of design, architecture, engineering, anthropology and work psychology, integrating a range of applied and academic perspectives. We interacted with participants and with each other in different ways, asking questions, making observations, conducting interviews, designing and installing workplace interventions, recording feedback – all to shed light on the workplace which older knowledge workers inhabit.

The study adopted a multi-method research design, which means that we tried to gain understanding in different ways. We asked questions in more and less formal structures and settings, one-to-one and in groups; we observed the environments that our workers were using and designed interventions in which participants could interact with new aspects of the work environment. We hoped to create opportunities for older workers to reflect on their experience and communicate with us about their work present, past and future. Our intention was to create richer insights into the complex interaction between older people, their work and their environment.

In designing our research methodology, above all we wanted to give older workers their own voice in relating their needs and preferences. We wanted to place the real experts about extended working lives centre stage to speak from their own experience. We were determined to engage older workers in defining the relevant areas to explore and the design interventions to test out – and to let them decide how and when they use the alternative work settings we created. We therefore deliberately did not extend the study to younger workers. No comparisons would be made between older workers and their younger colleagues – unless these comparisons were made by the older workers themselves.

Three global knowledge industries

As well as being multidisciplinary, the *Welcoming Workplace* study was also multinational – research was carried out in the UK, Japan and Australia. In these three countries we looked at knowledge workers in the pharmaceutical, technology and financial services industries, respectively. We went into the headquarters of large corporate global organisations – one each in the UK and Japan and two in Australia – who were generous enough to host our intensive 'case study' methodology. The organisations that opened their doors to us have a strong belief in the effect of the work environment on productivity and well-being. They wish to stay at the forefront of workplace design and provide their workers with the best environment to be effective and healthy. They are also now aware of changing demographics and the power of office design to attract and retain talent and expertise.

With the help of academic partners overseas, we repeated our questions, design interventions and workspace observations in these three countries because they sit along a spectrum of an ageing workforce in the developed world. As we outlined in Chapter 2, Japan, on one side of the spectrum, leads with the fastest-ageing population in the world; Australia has a relatively young work population within the developed world, but is ageing fast along the same demographic curve; and the UK is situated in between these two.

We expected that work environments in the different countries would vary in how they cater for older knowledge workers, as a function of where they stand on the ageing population spectrum. So we went in looking for differences. However what we discovered were marked similarities in older people's needs of their workplace and the degree to which these are universally not being catered for. Themes emerged that were common and consistent in all three locations, despite the differences in demographics, culture and industry.

How the study was undertaken

In each organisation, we met with the people responsible for the productivity and well-being of older knowledge workers – those who direct the HR strategy and environmental decisions, including senior managers in human resources, real estate, facilities, diversity and occupational health. In all, we conducted 14 in-depth interviews with these functional experts. Discussions focused on the organisation's work environment strategy, the needs of their older workers and any experiences of addressing these needs. The juxtaposition of the perceptions of older workers themselves and those responsible for their welfare provided some of the most intriguing insights of the study.

Through the companies' real-estate department, an e-mail was sent to 'experienced' employees with regards to participation in the study where they would be asked to give their perspective of their work environment. Response was higher than anticipated and participants were chosen on a practical availability and first-come basis. A total of 40 employees, men and women, in a variety of middle-management roles and functions, all over the age of 50 (the oldest aged 72), were interviewed. A two-hour, interviewee-led, semi-structured interview was conducted with each.

These interviews explored the participants' work skills and responsibilities, work patterns, use of the office environment, ergonomics and facilities, their health and their perceptions of the effects of ageing in relation to work, thoughts about retirement, and attitudes in the organisation towards older employees. The interviews were content-analysed and used to direct a technique called 'rapid design intervention', allowing the design researchers to create and rapidly install a set of experimental design settings that reflected and further tested key issues gleaned from interviews.

In this second phase of the study, three environments were designed which focused on core activities identified by the older knowledge workers as central to their work. These were named Collaboration, Concentration and Contemplation. The three environments were populated with design interventions based on insights from the interviews. Workers were invited to carry out their work in these new environments, throughout a period of up to two weeks, alone or with colleagues.

Sixty older workers, including those we interviewed, came along to try out the research environments, some returning many times. Participants were encouraged to perform their work in any of the new settings, which featured changes in lighting, acoustics, furniture, technology and ambience. Interaction with the environments was observed, and workers' feedback as to what they found helpful to their work and acceptable in the office environment, elicited and recorded both verbally and in written questionnaires.

In total, around 80 older workers took part in the *Welcoming Workplace* research, giving us ideas, sharing their long-held and new insights on their work environment, and directing our thinking about creating more welcoming office environments for the growing number of older knowledge workers. In the following chapters we describe and reflect on what we discovered.

10   Open plan has its limits

Concentration and confidentiality affected by being on parade

The corporate offices we encountered as part of the *Welcoming Workplace* research were typical of many organisations around the world – large, open-plan spaces for use by all but a top layer of management who work in cellular offices. The main function of the open plan is to accommodate the vast majority of knowledge workers and facilitate their productive work. In our study, we saw a range of knowledge workers including research chemists, process engineers and financial analysts at work in open plan.

This arrangement was perceived with some pride by those in charge, who saw it as reflecting a democratic, open and transparent culture allowing for the type of informal and organic communication and collaboration not possible in old-style offices. The breakdown of walls is equated with the breakdown of barriers and silos, facilitating the access and sharing of information and ideas so essential to the knowledge-based organisation. The fact that the open plan also caters to other business considerations, such as facilitating monitoring and control, and is driven above all by cost considerations, only serves to stoke the idealistic fervour of organisations to bring down the walls.

A deliberate plan to network

The open-plan areas we studied were supplemented with a variety of informally connected spaces aimed at giving workers choice and flexibility of environments to match different types of work. Closed-off meeting rooms complemented the open plan, providing a confidential teamwork environment while protecting the open plan from distraction. Other spaces such as breakout zones, cafeterias and reception areas were designed as semi-social spaces to entice workers to get up from their desks, stay on site, work, mingle and network. All were there as part of a plan to enhance collaboration with colleagues and visitors. They clearly reflect the strategic importance placed by these forward-looking organisations on communication, flow of information and networking.

From our interviews with the managers responsible for real estate, facilities, human resources and health, it was striking to note that, typically, older workers are more likely to express and exhibit difficulties with the open-plan environment. The quotes from older workers below are not unique, though some senior employees find such settings harder to cope with than others:

'The move was traumatic, leaving my big office and an admin person who supported me, and coming here to the open plan. I hated it. Took me three years to cope, caused me tension and aggravation.'

'I prefer to work in an office on my own, but that doesn't happen anymore. I had my own office... If you're adaptable, you manage.'

'It would be good to have an analysis of the cost of the open plan. What are the benefits of the open plan and at what cost; to have an easily compelling understood reason why I'm in an open plan. Then maybe I'd find it easier attitudinally to cope with it; there's an awful lot of resistance.'

'I can't do my job as effectively...so a lot of things then become a problem. You do have to do a lot of things at home because you have to catch up. Are we actually gaining from being public property, is that actually helping? Is it making people work particularly better? You're not in control if you're always interrupted...'

Also, typically, management will tend to view this as a sign of older workers' inability to adapt, change and embrace 'new ways of working'. Dangerously, any contention is brushed aside as standing in the way of inevitable change and progress. So strong and compelling is the trend towards open-plan working that, like a tsunami, it engulfs all things in its wake. As eager facilities managers told us:

> 'There are a lot of people who've been here a long time... in the old building they had a sense of exclusivity...Here intentionally you have lots of glass, which means you can be seen. They prefer their own little silo. But certainly not the young, they understand the new ways of working.'

> 'Some of the older workers are more resistant to floor plans; they are the people who sat in their offices with natural light. The MD led by example; if they don't want to come along, you drag them; it was a fairly tough process.'

Taking as a given that our host organisations seek to increase the productivity and well-being of their workers, and expecting that older workers themselves are concerned with their productivity and health, we took a fresh look at what older workers are actually saying about their work experience in the open-plan office. Are they expressing legitimate concerns about the working environment?

Collaboration versus concentration

We quickly learnt that the breakdown of walls and private spaces due to the focus on collaboration and teamwork has resulted in neglect of environments that promote 'solo' knowledge work. According to our older participants, the open-plan office (in tandem with alternative spaces provided) is mainly successful in facilitating the various forms of collaboration for which it is intended. Open plan is not however conducive to another host of essential knowledge-work tasks which depend on individual concentration.

Most of the demands associated with planning, analysis, creation, processing, problem solving and writing of complex information require uninterrupted and extended attention spans, and introverted thinking, a state of mind deemed difficult within the open-plan office. The majority of older workers we spoke to mentioned difficulties in concentration when working on these kinds of tasks, which to greater or lesser degrees are an absolutely essential part of their work. These quotes from older knowledge workers are typical:

> 'I find it hard to concentrate. My team can all be talking on the phone and I have to concentrate on a financial report. That was a challenge, and continues to be.'

> 'Nobody is making a lot of noise, but one is on the phone; another, someone has come up to him to discuss; usually it's about work; you could have eight conversations at a time.'

'I don't need to interact with my team on a daily basis, a function of the way I do it or my particular role. A lot of my work is concentrated, quiet work.'

'There is no space to concentrate. You can concentrate up to a point but it's very difficult to concentrate fully.'

Noise is the most significant and consistent cause of distraction. Interestingly, it is not only the level of the noise in the office that is distracting but the relative volume even in a relatively quiet office. While there is no denying that some over-hearing is important to the flow of information in the office, the specific content of conversations are probably the biggest contributors to the inability to concentrate. Spaces and environments change what people do at work. It is evident that a workplace that does not facilitate this crucial aspect of work risks reducing productivity, increasing mistakes and discouraging workers from attempting complex tasks in a non-conducive environment.

Older workers also told us that working in the open-plan office feels like being 'public property', 'on view' and 'on call' at all times. Whether this is the case with younger workers as well is a subject for another study. Anecdotal evidence suggests that younger workers may be more adept at multitasking and working in noisier environments. But with little control over an environment in which they need to accomplish tasks requiring longer and deeper concentration, all workers may sometimes struggle to concentrate to the extent that the task requires:

'There are times I find I'm irritated when people hold conversations with high voices, just like I do. Sometimes people are having some fun and it's essential in an office. We are opinionated and voices rise.'

'Because of work with professionals outside the office you are contacted anytime during the day. It's very difficult to manage free time...'

'Noise effects concentration. Non-work related noise is very distracting, snippets of conversation and laughing and joking. Sometimes the work is not so interesting and it's easy to be distracted...I very rarely ask for quiet.'

'My hearing is apparently too good. I sometimes play a CD when I want to read something technical or focus.'

Escaping to the home

Though no formal space is normally made available to directly facilitate concentration, people will not be defeated by design, and we discovered that our older workers will find empty offices and quiet corners to use on a haphazard basis, or they will stay at home and work, if that is possible. Work from home, away from the distractions of the open-plan office, is often the only way full concentration can be achieved. Part of the home is 'annexed' for work, and often assessed, fitted out and monitored by the company. Clearly, in the knowledge economy, more and more work is crossing the domestic threshold in the laptop bag.

Work from home compensates for the shortcomings of the open-plan office, and cynics may say that organisations are using their employees' homes as a free extension of their property to gain a type of environment that should be adequately provided for at work. Older workers, though, appear to enjoy working from home; importantly, it contributes to their motivation and loyalty. Yet work from home is invariably constricted by role, the need for face-to-face meetings and inadequate facilities for working in the home.

The pendulum swings back and forth between trust and autonomy on the one hand, and the limitations of supervisory management culture and the lingering requirement for monitoring, on the other. Company myths abound: the child answering the phone telling the manager that father is playing golf, or the CEO visiting the expensive office HQ and finding it almost completely empty of employees. The result is compromise and ambivalence towards working from home, which gives workers back the privacy they miss in those huge 'on parade' open-plan spaces but obscures them from view in terms of work supervision and, as we shall discover later, career advancement.

Hot-desking is a hot issue

Reorganisation of the office around the concept of hot-desking – under different guises such as 'the hotel concept' or 'the smart office' – was at various stages of introduction in the organisations we visited. Under these hot-desk arrangements, employees do not 'own' their own workstation but are allocated a space on a just-in-time basis; corporate seniority and status is not rewarded with fixed geographical territory in this new, more flexible world of working.

This trend is sure to grow due to the cost of real estate and pressures to utilise space more effectively. But as smaller office footprints are utilised more intensively, hot-desk areas are likely to become more crowded. Many of our older participants told us that they judge hot-desking to be bad for concentration – but also with a detrimental impact on collaboration; in other words, offering the worst of both worlds. Most noted that hot-desking arrangements break up teams that would normally sit in proximity and would more conventionally create a community of shared practice, disrupting the rhythm of teamwork and making life hard for managers too.

Management brushes aside these concerns, insisting that hot-desking will promote communication between workers who are less likely to meet otherwise, and that technology and modern output-based management techniques no longer necessitate the need for managers to site their team physically next to them. Indeed the argument is advanced that you don't even need to know when or where team members get the job done. Since the increase of mobile and multi-site work arrangements on the one hand, and cost considerations on the other make the rapid rise of hot-desking inevitable, the organisation clearly needs to convince and train its older managers in these new ways of managing. As one complained to us: 'The adjacency of the team helps the team with understanding, communication flow, cuts down need for meetings. So I was resistant to moving...'

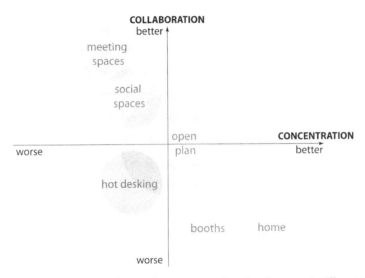

Chart showing framework created to map perception of performance in different types of workspace (Welcoming Workplace, 2008)

Mapping out the provision of space

To get a better handle on all of these issues, we created a framework to map out the provision of different types of workspace for knowledge workers using two variables – perception of their effect on collaboration (better to worse) and perception of their effect on concentration (better to worse). We placed the standard open-plan office at the centre of the map as the neutral common denominator. It immediately became graphically clear that, in current practice, many more spaces are allocated for collaborative work, whether social areas or meeting rooms, and that there is a dearth of space catering properly for solo, concentrated work. Hot-desking was perceived as reducing the effectiveness of both team-based and solo 'quiet' work. Home-working was seen as ideal for concentrated work but with the inevitable detrimental effect on collaborative endeavours.

Open-plan office design emerged from our study as supporting work that requires a short attention span, multitasking and constant communication. In strategy, it is aligned with principles of democratisation and transparency, but for specific tasks this environment can reduce effectiveness and increase mistakes. Older workers may be in the vanguard of those exhibiting the difficulties of concentration in the open-plan office but we believe the issue is more inclusive – the provision of quiet concentration space within modern offices would benefit all and would generally increase the quality of knowledge work.

A problem with confidentiality

While concentration is a big problem, so too is the issue of confidentiality. We know from the experience of quarrelling academics at Sussex University's Freeman Centre (see Chapter 6) that confidentiality can be easily compromised in open plan. The *Welcoming Workplace* participants told us that such arrangements do not support confidential work, which is part of their role as knowledge workers and managers. Where within the open-plan office does one have confidential work meetings or carry out essential confidential work as an individual? Here is a selection of comments:

> '*Here there is a shortage of offices for confidential discussions, issues to do with something on site that's confidential, in my line of work.*'

> '*The agitation of finding a room for a confidential discussion...*'

> '*It's hard to manage a team, with all the personal development stuff, without an office, whereas there are people with no management responsibilities with an office.*'

> '*You tend to do classified work early in the morning when no one is around.*'

> '*There's more need for security, you don't know who's coming up behind you.*'

> '*I make some work calls which I prefer people not hear. Often you are talking about people... about performance or whatever... You go somewhere with your mobile.*'

It seems that in the rush to break down walls, confidential work has become synonymous with non-transparent, non-productive work. Closed-off spaces are assumed by management to be misused for private, non-legitimate purposes; they are covert and difficult to monitor. Again the pendulum swings between trust and surveillance. As one manager told us: 'People want their own space because they can control it – phone their girlfriend – usually negative reasons.'

Confidential work – both on one's own and with colleagues – has become an underrated aspect of knowledge work; it is both insufficiently catered for and not encouraged in the workplace. As a consequence no formal spaces are provided for confidential work and workers cope with makeshift and unsatisfactory solutions. This, of course, impacts negatively on the changing workforce: it might be the case that engagement with confidential and developmental work is avoided due to the openness of the environment.

11 Fit for purpose?

Health and well-being under strain in the workplace

While the older workers we studied in UK, Japan and Australia struggled with particular aspects of open-plan working, they overwhelmingly regarded themselves as fit and well to do so. They reported that they keep 'in shape' to various degrees and were conscious of the benefits of being active to compensate for largely sedentary and stressful working lives within knowledge-based organisations. They go to the gym, bicycle or walk to work, often take the stairs in preference to the lift, and embark on various active pursuits, in and out of the office. They also believe that work keeps them in good stead, sharp and alert mentally as they age:

> 'Depends where in the cycle of fitness I am whether I use the stairs. I try to.'

> 'I don't play ball sports, the thought of going on a treadmill in the gym drives me to distraction. If I want exercise I'd go up and down the stairs. I trained for a trip in the Alps like that.'

> 'I also do the gym two mornings a week. I'd like to do different activities. I've always been sporty.'

Nevertheless, alongside descriptions of good health and active pursuits, the older workers we interviewed were quick to acknowledge the physical changes with ageing. A weakening of sight, tiredness and 'aches and pains' were mentioned most frequently. Though in no way debilitating, these symptoms form a backdrop to older peoples' work, necessitating constant and effective self-management.

Most significantly, the symptoms experienced by older workers increase their sensitivity to and dependence on the physical work environment. They require better light to see by, and may become more particular about the chair they sit on. Coping and compensating strategies are evident with age, such as using wheeled bags for carrying laptops or reading from print in a large font in preference to on screen. Here are some typical comments:

'Got the usual aches and pains, depends on length of time in chair; an ache in the hips; if I notice it, I get up, you mustn't be sedentary for too long.'

'Certainly sight is weaker. I have to wear glasses for reading now, but then I can't look at the computer screen, it's blurry. Maybe the answer is a bigger screen. And the light sometimes seems to disturb. I open and close the shades a lot.'

'I know from myself, my energy or focus have diminished with age.'

'I've got one pair of glasses for the computer, one for long-distance vision, one for outdoors and one for driving.'

In the open-plan office and its associated communal spaces, employees control very little of their environment. The features of the open-plan environment, including light, temperature, acoustics and furniture, no matter how good, cater to the most common and standard needs – and tend to be controlled centrally.

'That's the problem in open-plan offices, it's an average environment for average people, in terms of light, heat, everything.'

'The environment of light in the open-plan office is not right...row upon row of ceiling lights, like an open shed; the lights don't line up with the desks.'

'The lights are turned off for energy saving during lunch breaks. On days with bad weather it becomes pitch-black. I go by the window and read. During lunch breaks I work in the dark.'

'The biggest issue I have is with too much light. I put on sunglasses, pull the blinds. With light reflecting off the screen, sometimes you can't see what's written.'

'The lighting is inconsistent. Is my view, it's quite dark. But I've worked in hellish buildings, so I can't complain.'

'I find I need more light. I've seen lots of people not using it and I think what's wrong with me, but I need more light to read efficiently, I'm ten years older than them.'

A need for alternatives

Within open-plan space, knowledge work is equated with sitting down. We saw a variety of office furniture in terms of style and quality, but the consistent feature was sitting at a desk. To get up from your seat signals a stop to doing serious work. Design can provide a variety of alternative work postures and positions, enabling work in perching, semi-reclining and stand-up positions, for example, which could benefit older workers enormously, and possibly prevent work-related skeletal-muscular complaints when used by younger workers as well. But there were few alternatives on view. As one worker explained: 'I've been working and sitting for 35 years. If you're sitting for that length of time, you feel yourself compacting…it becomes a health issue.'

Given that older workers are more sensitive to and reliant on their physical and ergonomic environment, standardised open plan fails to cater for their needs and preferences because there is no capacity for personalisation and change. This is the classic double bind for an ageing workforce of the low-segmentation, low-choice office – it's not right in the first place and you can't alter it.

It is known that muscular-skeletal disorders are on the increase, including repetitive strain injury and back pain, and that they constitute the most frequent health problem for older workers. It is also known, as we established in Chapter 8, that older eyes need more light and older ears cannot filter out background noise from useful sounds as effectively. The symptoms of ageing suggest that proactive workplace design could help older workers manage their environment better, and benefit their productivity and well-being. Yet none of the workplaces we visited were proactive in terms of monitoring, understanding or planning for age-related needs.

Problems with shared space

The ergonomic squeeze on older knowledge workers is further exacerbated by the roles and privileges they acquire over time inside the organisation. As we know, these are the people more likely to be working on special assignments or part time in recognition of their experience and expertise, or contributing in other flexible ways. As a result they may not have a permanent desk in the office but will rely on those shared-space and hot-desk scenarios that are the most difficult to get right ergonomically.

It is one of the ironies of the contemporary office that the group of premium employees most dependent on a quality environment and least able to cope with poorly considered hot-desks should be the prime candidates for such arrangements. Design for shared spaces emerged as a priority from our study.

Rest and recuperation

We have established that current office design can be uncomfortable and tiring for an ageing workforce. But activities such as recuperation and restoration are not typically associated with the corporate work environment – and are in fact an anathema to it. Whether you are at the desk or in 'breakout areas', it is difficult to be seen not to be working. Our observations of the workplace suggest that it is designed for fully functioning and fully active individuals, with no space set aside for inactivity and rest.

Many modern employers do prioritise active fitness in various ways, but the design and culture of most organisations is still oblivious to the recuperative nature of rest from active pursuits. Older workers we interviewed told us that they sneaked into the nurse's room for a lie down and that they felt at times hindered by tiredness. The workplace simply does not cater for recuperation and restoration, an omission that particularly affects the over-50s, as these comments suggest:

> 'I get tired and I don't mean physical. I get sleepy at the end of the day, around 4pm when I'm doing boring things I need to do.'

> 'I need to turn off for half an hour in the middle of the day. I'm not comfortable stopping for something non-related to work here.'

> 'If I started showing less energy, people would start considering me older. But I'm high on energy and people see me like that.'

> 'There's nowhere you can be away to think and away from everyone. We have the glass meeting rooms but you're exposed. It would be nice to be somewhere where you're not exposed. Just for five minutes...'

When considering the needs of older knowledge workers, it is important to recognise the varying pace of the body throughout the day, which may include states of low energy. In the right environment, short periods of 'contemplation', 'meditation' or 'power napping' may boost work-related mental activity and productivity among all employees, not just older ones, resulting in a re-energised, happier and healthier workforce. Resting within the workplace increases an overall sense of well-being, lessens stress and may lead to a decrease in days away from work. Office design, as we shall explain in Section 3 of this book, can be creative and inclusive in catering for this need for restoration, so that younger employees make as much use of such facilities as older colleagues.

However, before office design can apply its practical touch, there needs to be a cultural shift in the perception of work and rest as opposites occupying the workplace and the home respectively and exclusively. We believe that just as work has entered the home and appropriated space and time, so rest, refuge and recuperation functions associated with the home should now be allowed to take up space in the workplace. A space within the workplace could act as 'home away from home' to allow rest and reflection, and improve both productivity and health. As working lives extend, a change of culture is needed to allow older workers to listen to their own bodies and maintain their health and well-being. Otherwise the burnout is complete – mental and physical.

12 Trapped inside the box

How new technology stifles techniques honed over time

If the limitations of office ergonomics pose a physical challenge to the productivity and well-being of older workers, then consider how information technology plays with their heads. Such technology is synonymous with knowledge work on the basis of sharing information and transforming ways of working. But in many cases technology acts to exclude older workers in a way similar to how physical strength once acted as the barrier to manual work for ageing blue-collar employees. Ironically, white-collar office work was expected to put older workers on a more equal footing and allow them to remain working for longer.

A pervasive perception of older knowledge workers is that they are lagging in essential IT skills. In our research, we constantly heard this sentiment expressed by management. As one manager put it, 'Technology is the future, but it is based on the younger generation'. These beliefs about a lack of facility with the key new skills of information and communication technologies threaten to make older knowledge workers obsolete and to erase as irrelevant the advantages of experience, knowledge and maturity.

We tried to get under the skin of this perception about lagging behind in technology skills. Older participants in the study talked to us about their experiences within technology-based organisations; about their relationship with technology; and about whether their organisations were doing enough to increase their technology skills as required. On the whole, the workers we spoke to believed they possessed the technology skills adequate for the role they are performing. Some felt they were starting from a lower base of confidence than their younger colleagues, while others pointed out that they have been dealing with computer technology in all its developmental stages for decades. Here are some typical comments:

> *'There is a high technology, high level of capability throughout, including older workers.'*

> *'We went from word processors to computers, to lap-tops, and we learnt and adapted.'*

'Have been using computers since the word processing days...I don't find IT skills difficult.'

'I would ask if I get frustrated, but won't let it defeat me.'

'The last ten years, being involved in a massive project enabled me to learn new IT skills, to learn so much more.'

Most importantly, older workers took it for granted that they needed to develop their skills continuously and were confident of their ability to learn as required. This finding not only echoed the Finnish Work Ability concept and its emphasis on mental capacity sharpening with age (see Chapter 4) but also reflected the basic premise of a learning organisation. Being an expert is not a stable characteristic – a knowledge worker needs to learn and develop expertise continuously.

Staying abreast of technological change

In order to keep on top of relevant technology and use it to best effect, older workers told us that they enlist colleagues, help-desks, face-to-face training, e-training, sons and daughters and even grandchildren. They are open and adept at finding the solutions and information they need, as these comments suggest:

'IT training, you do it all the time. You have to learn to use new things. I have no problem keeping up.'

'IT support, I'd ask some of the guys how you do something or the help-desk. I'm not a great IT person. Sometimes a secretary will show me how to do something; if I haven't done it for a while, I forget.

'I'm not a computer geek, quite the reverse. I use the in-house training, the desktop support, I use my colleagues; if I hit a problem I know who has the expertise I don't.'

'If you don't understand something and ask a younger member of staff, they sometimes teach you...I try to take in new things like they are games.'

'They showed us how to use the phones in small groups, hands on. They did that quite well. You practised.'

However for all the support that can be enlisted, a minority of older workers reported that the help and training they receive is insufficient:

'From my perspective, they've become very bad at technology training here. If they introduce anything new, they don't train. Things arrive at your desk. Maybe there's an e-module, but I'm not going to that.'

'Even the mobile phone, nobody tells you how to make best use of it. When it rings, I answer it. Young people have taught me to text. Should somebody here have taught me? I learn slowly and only the functions I need. Nobody has taken the time to show me...They're not proactive...They could do more.'

'The IT department often sends new instructions for databases, but they are difficult to understand. You don't know what to do. You have to phone up or ask someone who knows.'

'You are expected to learn all the new software pretty much yourself. I'm old fashioned, it's nice to get taught. The young are ahead of us to be fair, they've grown up with it.'

'They say to me, it's easy. I say, maybe to you. If you come in and give me ten minutes I'll learn it, but if you don't I'll struggle with it.'

Clearly, new approaches are needed given the reliance of knowledge worker productivity on accessing information technology, and on occasions we did see examples of good practice. In the main entrance of our host corporation in Australia, a technology help-desk is situated to accommodate all queries and requests from workers young and old. The statement made by having such a prominent and accessible help-desk is that people will need support with technology, and that to seek help is transparent and legitimate, and to be expected.

This face-to-face, in-your-face approach was highly valued by the older workers we met, many of whom prefer to be less reliant on formal and standardised group training and e-training modules. Older workers also spoke about appreciating training that takes their particular level of technological agility and learning pace into account, as well as allowing a facility for follow-up queries. The message was clear: most of all, older workers want to learn technology skills that are relevant, and want to learn it on-the-job, as their task requires.

As we discussed in Chapter 3, research has proven that older people will retire later if there is a positive correlation between technological change and on-the-job training; but in our own study we saw no proactive attempts on the part of the organisations we visited to adjust the resources or methods of technology training to the specific needs of an ageing workforce. Such developments would raise the confidence of older workers and raise the organisation's confidence in its older workers, but cultural barriers appear to hinder their emergence.

Struggles with self-sufficiency

Often what seems as reluctance by older workers to take on new technology skills has little to do with the technology itself and a lot to do with what this demographic group see as a change in their role description and in the use of their expertise. New ways of working dictate a higher degree of self-sufficiency, which is facilitated by technology, including the requirement to take on new administrative tasks. Often, the higher up the hierarchy, the least chance the older worker has had of learning to cope without secretarial backup. These quotes describe the current position:

'If you consider the journey: 15 years ago we all had a secretary, we're not allowed to call them that now. It's now considered good use of a high manager's time to stand by the photocopier, prepare presentations, go online to buy a specialist computer bag. It's not ageist, it's a complete change of culture...I organised an event – a gross misuse of my time.'

'I think, is that what they pay me to do? I don't have admin support so I need to know calendars, databases, and so on myself. I need to be more self-sufficient, book my own car, meetings; with technology enabling, that's the trend. I'm resistant; it takes so much time. I'm not working as hard as I used to because there are so many aspects, for example, it took me ages to set up a big meeting.'

These changes to roles and responsibilities have even more impact when set alongside the negative effects of the ageing process on the basic ability to access technology, to use screens and mobile devices. Participants in our study reported problems with hearing, sight and dexterity in this respect:

'I don't text, it's too cumbersome. I'm happy for people to send me texts, but don't expect one back, I've got big fingers.'

'I'd like the monitor to be more flexible, with middle-age eyesight, I spend far too much time looking at the screen...if I'm tired, my eyes get tired, I'll leave my desk and get a coffee and do a crossword puzzle.'

Organisations need to focus on ways to counteract such problems – a little design thinking can make a big difference. Microsoft's Accessibility Business Unit claims that many of the technologies that can improve the experience of senior workers are already in existence, but older people are often unaware of these and their employers do not make the best job of customising technology for their needs.

Older workers are also selective about their communication medium of choice, partly because they may not have the facility or agility of use, but also because the media is the message and some forms of communication suit them better than others. Our study revealed a view among older workers that there are clear generational differences in use of the telephone, e-mail and instant messaging, for example.

'E-mail is my least preferred; I find it a bind, impersonal, and therefore I delay. It's clumsy and people are measured by how fast they respond.'

'I'm much more a people's person than a technical person. I'll never send an e-mail when I can ask face to face.'

'With e-mail the words become short. They do not like long messages. It is better to spend the time writing a short e-mail followed by a phone call. There are some who prefer the phone over e-mail. You adjust to the other person. But long telephone conversations are tiring.'

'I dislike communication via e-mail...it is difficult to grasp a person's ideas, feelings and emotions with e-mail. You rely only on written words with no intonations. You are not trained in how to write e-mails. Some may write them like letters and some informally, like they were speaking. E-mail is good for recording, but if you make a mistake using it, it can feel unpleasant.'

'I never use text, or instant messaging. Young people get more out of mobile phones. Probably over use them.'

'People of our generation, if we call somebody up we can wrap it up in five minutes, whereas e-mail would take half an hour. What's the point of back and forth? Just get on the phone.'

Must technology always be the answer?

Better design and more proactive guidance in the use of specific technological functions such as complex mobile phones or online diaries for administration would, we believe, help to build confidence and bridge the gap between older workers and new technology. But there is a more fundamental issue around technology that must be addressed – this is the determinist notion that technology must always be the ultimate tool of the knowledge worker and that modern knowledge-office design must always accommodate its use.

This perspective regards any alternative ways of working to screen and keyboard, mouse and pad, mobile, laptop and BlackBerry – the technology tools that completely fill the knowledge worker's desk – as anachronistic, unviable and irrelevant. This state of affairs is formalised by 'paperless office' and 'clean-desk' policies, a removal of storage space and the inability to display anything except via technology screens.

According to our participants, the corporate organisation assumes that there is only one way of working and learning, that everything a knowledge worker needs should be coming 'out of the box' in front of them. The design of the open-plan working environment reflects this fundamentalist view. At present the expectation is that older workers will adapt to technology-driven ways of working. Any hesitation or objection is attributed to age-related resistance to change. Older knowledge workers consistently reject this assumption and cite other reasons for their reluctance:

> *'This office is a one size fits all way of working. It assumes that people will go to the intranet.'*

'It's an assumption that one-size-fits-all solutions, never mind what you're doing, what role, what job, what level of seniority. But in some jobs there are tasks and pressures that the open plan clearly doesn't meet.'

'The intellectual level here is high. Everyone has different learning styles.'

'Tables could be bigger...I've got a keyboard, laptop, flat screen, telephone, mouse and pad. So not much room left for actual work.'

'The notion that offices are paperless is nonsense. I bet it's the same or more than it was: notes, reports, copies of e-mails. If working on a project, I'd keep key documents in a folder to take to meetings. It's all on my laptop but paper is quicker and easier than showing the laptop.'

Some are emphatic that to be optimally productive they need to work in alternative ways, which involve working beyond and outside the computer screen. Current workplace design, they claim, does not accommodate their alternative ways of working. These have been developed, tried and tested, and honed over many years to optimise their productivity, reflecting their longevity in the workplace. The quotes below reveal how they often feel their productivity is compromised:

'I work in an open-plan office and loathe it; just doesn't suit my way of working; I work visually; they think everything is on the little screen...I work suboptimal, I would say.'

'Age has a bearing on how much paper you store on your desk. It's because of my work habits; I'm not using the computer as much as I should perhaps. I need more shelving all the time, and more desk space; need to have it all there within sight.'

Alternatives to the screen

Older workers told us that they would benefit from alternatives to screen-based work for creating, processing and storing information. They mentioned visual displays to stimulate or structure their thoughts, backdrops and walls to hang graphs and charts, facilities that allow spreading out blocks of text and representations of data in ways which the screen does not allow, and storage for hardcopies, books and manuals. They might be termed 'messy', 'visual' or 'spreaders' by managers, but it became clear that our participants require different workspaces and fixtures not offered in their open workspace if they are to capitalise on their optimal ways of working, honed over a long career.

'Nice to have a project on the wall...here to put things on walls, if you can find walls, you have to go through long procedures. It's a clean-desk policy.'

'I prefer to print documents off than reading on the screen. I find it restricting to see it bit by bit.'

'There's no library, no reference books which we used to have.'

For most of the older knowledge workers we spoke to, the shift to working in an open-plan office from a cellular office has taken place relatively recently – and fairly late in their working lives. Most, but not all, had occupied their own office or small, shared office. The physical move to open plan and the cultural shift associated with open plan has left them needing to adapt very rapidly to significantly different ways of working. Contrary to the stereotype that casts older workers as inflexible and unable to adapt to new ways of working, we found that older workers are the ones changing and adapting more than anyone else.

Productivity not optimised

The total focus on the computer screen in the open-plan office has meant that ways of working developed over many years to optimise productivity have been given up. The restrictions on alternative ways of working – such as clean-desk policies – have disempowered older workers disproportionately. Based on a lifetime's accumulation of working practices, most acquired in the pre-digital era, older knowledge workers need space away from the computer screen to spread out, hang up and make a mess. It is interesting to note that what older workers demand in this context is akin to contemporary design concepts for facilitating creativity and innovation with pin-up areas, romp rooms and so on. This leads us to suggest that facilitation of alternative ways of working in a more 'visual office' would benefit all working in open plan. We shall go on to describe some these facilities in Section 3 of this book.

It may well be that very productive and creative ways of working held by older employees, but effective for everyone, are being discarded simply because of who is advocating them. Older workers may not be resistant to change, so much as have legitimate concerns about change. In the next chapter, we go on to explore the issue right at the heart of rethinking the culture – institutional attitudes to ageing within the organisation.

13 Ambivalence to ageing

Institutional uncertainty and bias form a backdrop to working lives

In the large and progressive companies that hosted the *Welcoming Workplace* research and welcomed us into their facilities, it was difficult to pinpoint bias. Such anti-age discrimination regulations and policies that had been introduced were accepted with surprise or indifference. Senior employees were quick to confirm that there was no overt discrimination in company protocols and regulations against older workers. They stated that they worked in enlightened companies operating a fair approach evident in selection, promotion and training practices. Here are some of their positive comments:

> *'I can't think we need age discrimination laws here; maybe in a less aware company; we're very good.'*

> *'To be honest, when I saw these age rules and new legislation I was surprised. If my job was more physical maybe it would get more difficult as you get older. I've never felt (I was) stopped from going on training because someone younger has gone instead.'*

> *'No age divide in this building, there's such a wide age range here.'*

> *'There's no age discrimination in the company. I applied for two jobs and didn't get them but I don't relate it to age.'*

Left there, we would conclude that bias and prejudice have no detrimental effect on those older workers who are holders of knowledge, experienced contributors to their company's productivity, and who are lucky enough to be working in properly managed organisations. (The only exceptions to this state of affairs were found in Japan where retirement regulations force managers to retire in their early 50s after which many are brought back to work on short-term contracts in an environment fraught with uncertainty.)

However, listening closely as our participants share more of their daily experience of being an older knowledge worker, it became clear to us that they exist in a milieu that we can only describe as 'institutional ambivalence'. Ambivalent messages about the extent to which their skills are of value, uncertainty about whether the company is attempting to facilitate their stay or their exit, decreases in status and lack of access to promotions, form an unnerving backdrop to the daily activities of the ageing workforce.

Past culls cast a shadow

Even at a time when market forces favour older workers and governments are campaigning to keep them working longer, ambivalence in organisations appears to be rife. On the one hand, older workers know their organisation must retain them; it is harder to recruit younger people and it is difficult to replace the skills and knowledge that they possess, especially the traditional skills in such areas as engineering that are scarce in the younger generation. Losing mature and experienced employees, they reason, is a brain drain to the organisation.

On the other hand, they are often uncertain about the relevance of their skills and expertise, and only too aware that organisations have, in the recent past, made sweeping culls of older workers through early retirement and redundancy as part of reorganisation processes – culls which, being younger then, they just managed to escape. The model is there for dispensing with older workers when the going gets tough. It is sometimes held up as a natural and ethical model: the old making room for the young; those who have had their chance giving way to those who have not.

In addition, skills in technology are a major bouncer, and older workers are not likely to be seen as 'the future of the company' in which to invest resource, training and development. Depending to a degree on their rank, function and nationality, older workers interviewed for our research expressed varying degrees of anxiety about their standing in the 'ambivalent' organisation:

> *'New systems are revised all the time, Processes and IT systems change, and so turnover helps the business along.'*

> *'Low turnover rate was an issue; the staff had stayed so long; moving into a progressive (open-plan) building they were hoping would help their turnover (of staff).'*

> *'People with expertise who have been in the business a long time are the most expensive for the business and therefore best cost-reduction in reorganisations.'*

> *'Speaking from an engineering perspective, there is a skills shortage in the young workforce; no apprentices; often the young British don't take up mechanical or electrical; skills only exist with the older workers.'*

> *'It's different for older people in senior jobs, but in mid-management level they assume you weren't excellent because you didn't move fast enough through the organisation.'*

Such ambivalence to ageing workers begins to seep through the organisation affecting prospects for training, promotion and other types of career advancement, as participants told us in confidence:

> *'I speak to older colleagues and, we agree, we are no longer on the fast track to anywhere. It doesn't surprise me.'*

> *'When you get to your 50s the treatment received is different; what is expected of you is different; you can still grow in your 40s but the 50s are a collecting, regathering period; the wage structure changes and you don't get promoted; motivation gets lowered.'*

> *'There have been many older people who were seen as "slowing down" the company.'*

> *'There was to be a policy around encouraging us to stay longer…but I haven't seen this policy in play.'*

> *'We had a discussion yesterday about older people applying for internal jobs and they don't even get a look in.'*

Stereotypes shape relationships

Even with the rise in age awareness in recent years, age discrimination in the workplace seems to be where we were with stereotypes of women 20 years ago. Ageism is widespread and institutional. Older workers experience a set of stereotypically biased expectations that seem to have been modified to make them more pertinent to the current workplace. Though employers acknowledge some of the positive characteristics associated with ageing, such as an ability to establish and maintain networks of clients and colleagues, they also attributed many negative characteristics and attitudes – 'resistance to change' being especially relevant to the workplace.

Change is a constant feature of organisational life and, as we have discussed in earlier chapters of this book, knowledge-led companies demand the flexibility and quick response required to meet shifting global market demands. As a result, greater emphasis is placed on the ability of workers to adapt to change and learn new skills quickly. Being classified as an older worker means – in a coded way – being perceived as less flexible and less adaptable, more difficult to manage, and slower to take on new ways of working and adapt to change. These stereotypes, in effect, mean older workers as a group are seen to lack the essential capabilities that make modern organisations competitive. Employers then judge older workers in terms of their stereotypical capabilities rather than on their true merit.

In addition, negative stereotypes are known to be assimilated into the self-concept of older people and to negatively impact their own confidence in their abilities. Furthermore, older workers are very aware of these negative perceptions, which tend to colour their behaviour and relationships with their colleagues and managers, as these comments reveal:

> 'The young are passionate, keen, vibrant. Any new people are a breath of fresh air. As I say, there are a lot of people who've been here a long time…'

> 'People probably see me as stuck in my ways – "she's very experienced but she has her own ways of doing things", that is the subtext.'

> 'People of my age are more expensive, we have pensions and benefits. They probably would like to get rid of me…I look at it from a business perspective and I think I need to look after myself. It's affecting me; I won't have certain conversations with my manager.'

> 'There is a perception that age has to do with inflexibility and inability to learn; I'm not saying every single person thinks this, but there is a general perception of "what are we going to do with the old workforce?" That's the culture we need to do something about.'

In this context, we discovered there is a high price to pay for being signalled out as an older worker and for expressing particular needs or special requirements. Therefore, it was not surprising to learn that older workers do not want to be identified as a 'special needs' group at work, even though they do have special needs in terms of ergonomics and design which would, if addressed, be hugely beneficial to the productivity of the organisation:

'I don't look my age; I'm not open about my age; when you tell your age they start looking at you with a new set of lenses, whether it's conscious or not. ...I see them preparing for my exit. And it is getting to me a bit.'

'We are at the age we are and we'll get older. I never expected to be dealt with differently. They don't think I'm the age I am, I try to hide it. It's not about looks, it's about attitude.'

'...with my trendy tights, you colour your hair, you're covering up.'

No special thought for ageing

Not only do older workers actively avoid being identified as 'older', the managers responsible for their welfare are complicit in this stance. The organisations we studied showed modern and enlightened traits in terms of their grasp of the relationship between environment, productivity and well-being of their workers. On the whole they provide their employees with state-of-the-art open-plan offices, communal spaces, furnishings and training in use of the environment. Yet, from our interviews with the HR, real estate and facilities experts who manage the requirements of employees, including those hurtling towards retirement age, it became clear that none of the organisations gives special thought to the specific needs of its older workers when planning and designing the workplace.

Older workers are expected to fit in, as they mostly do. Their managers assume, quite correctly, that older workers would not welcome being singled out as older. They fear the impact on workplace relations and even the possible legal implications of distinguishing a group of workers as older. They believe that an ageing workforce is any case catered for indirectly by design for disability:

'There are obviously ergonomic differentials. All buildings have to be designed with disability in mind. If you were old, you would benefit from that.'

'As you get older you don't perceive yourself as any different, you see a 19-year-old looking back in the mirror. They won't regard themselves as a special needs group.'

Where inclusive design fits in

This state of affairs makes it difficult to target older workers proactively with design initiatives, adding further to the sense of ambivalence around ageing in the workplace. However, this is where inclusive design has a role to play. A central tenant of inclusive design is that by focusing on the needs of 'extreme' users, design can be made more accessible for all. The implication for older knowledge workers is clear. Adhering to inclusive design principles will make it easier for managers to plan – and for older workers to accept – important interventions that will benefit all with a more productive and healthy office design.

14 Responding to the challenge

Time to design: habitat and behaviour are linked

From the glass towers on London's Great West Road to the grey office blocks of Yokohama and Melbourne's waterside financial district, our research with older workers inside knowledge-led organisations left us with plenty to ponder. The participants in the *Welcoming Workplace* study on three continents articulated clearly the need to rethink the culture that surrounds ageing in the workplace. Interviews and observations led us to the conclusion that for all their progressive intent, strategies for new ways of working in the open-plan environment leave many senior employees struggling to cope.

We identified cultural barriers everywhere. We saw those keynotes of knowledge work, concentration and confidentiality, badly affected by one-size-fits-all design, and evidence of *faux* collaboration based simply on geographical proximity rather than the provision of dedicated settings for teamworking. Spaces to think, ponder and recuperate from the daily grind – a kind of oasis for contemplation or escape – were largely absent from consideration. But then even basic attention to the needs of an ageing workforce was missing. Both older workers and the experts managing their welfare were complicit in staying silent.

The special sensitivity and dependence that older workers feel towards their environment was not really acknowledged, affecting health and well-being. Training in information technology was often inappropriately managed and an absolute reliance on screen-based work was viewed as unhelpful by professionals who have spent much of their career honing their skills and optimising their productivity in the era before digital technology swept all before it. Above all, there is a kind of unseen institutional bias within even the most humane organisations that manifests itself in uncertainty and ambivalence about the value of an ageing workforce.

Given this picture, how can corporate attitudes undergo transformation? One of the clearest and most visible ways to achieve this is to use a redesign of the physical workplace as a lever to change organisational culture. The proven link between habitat and behaviour has been well established by anthropologists over many years. More recently, the American academic Franklin Becker has written about 'organisational ecology' – the symbiotic relationship between the social organism of the organisation and the internal physical structure of the environment within which it breathes and mutates. Few company leaders today would choose to initiate a programme of change management – for example, from closed to open styles of governance or towards flatter hierarchies – without at least some mirroring or underpinning in the physical design of the workspace. This explains why there has been so much restless experiment in office design in recent years.

In this section we have looked at the barriers to rethinking the culture and, guided by our expert users, begun to address the range of solutions that can better support older knowledge workers. In the final section of the book, we go on to look at models for intervening in office space and redesigning the environment, so that the challenge of a changing workforce becomes an opportunity to innovate, not a brake on progress.

Part Three
Redesigning the environment

'We aim to allow the individual to work within an understandable landscape and on a familiar scale, a human workplace offering a variety of possibilities...'

Sevil Peach, Office Designer

15 Plotting your moves

Which design interventions are right for your company?

You have reviewed the context for knowledge work and an ageing workforce. You have looked at ways to rethink the culture of your organisation to give older knowledge workers a new deal in the new-style twenty-first century economy. Now, in the final section of this book, you are ready to confront the crux of the matter – redesigning the work environment to create a better fit for your changing workforce.

But wait, we hear you say: aren't offices fast losing their relevance in the networked economy? Isn't work becoming less dependent on place, and becoming more mobile, diffuse and multi-sited in character thanks to information technology? Isn't redesigning fixed office space to accommodate extended working lives a lesser priority than plugging the expertise of older workers into more flexible and casual patterns of work?

Do big corporate offices have a future?

Our answer is to point to the weight of current evidence showing that, despite advances in technology and the emergence of new ways of working, office buildings are not yet obsolete. On the contrary, the physical work environment appears as important as ever to how organisations perform, an anchor point for people to congregate. The nature of office work may be changing, but millions of people still flock to the workplace everyday. Office property still forms the backdrop to most working lives.

Given our continuing organisation of work around buildings, even if there is less singular attachment to place and more belief in complex networks than before, we are required to check our stride into the future. The central quest thus shifts in focus from finding alternatives to the office environment to finding ways to make such environments flex more successfully to meet a changing workforce.

When asked by *Building Design* magazine whether the big corporate office still had a future, architect and theorist Frank Duffy argued: 'There is going to be a lot more intellectual "office-like" activity in the knowledge economy...The consequence of the changing nature of work is that we may end up with too many conventional mono-functional office buildings which are massively underused...My bet is it would be safer to respond by refurbishing existing office space and using it more intensively.'

Duffy's assertion that office interior redesign and refurbishment will be key to matching the demands of knowledge economy with the activities and capabilities of the workforce is in line with our own position on this subject. In the main we don't need to build yet more conventional office buildings – we need to make more effective, productive and imaginative use of those we already have. We need to think differently about the corporate workplace from the point of view of planning and design. So where can design make an intervention?

Environmental changes make a difference

Review of the *Welcoming Workplace* project and other research studies leads us to some familiar targets: acoustics, lighting, information technology, furniture, ergonomics and ambience. (We hope and assume these will be familiar given the evidence we have marshalled earlier in this book.) By making relatively small changes within the environment, we believe there can be a disproportionately big impact on the productivity and comfort of older workers.

To test our convictions, we swiftly analysed the results of our interviews and observations as part of the *Welcoming Workplace* study and built a series of three experimental design settings inside the organisations hosting the research: one for aiding concentration, one for facilitating collaboration and a third for providing escape in the form of a contemplation space. These prototype environments were typically fabricated and installed within a week of the interviews being concluded, enabling research participants to work in them for an hour or a whole day if they wished.

This tactic of rapid design intervention gave us the opportunity to engage with our lead users – 80 in all, in the UK, Japan and Australia – at a deeper, more experiential level. By keeping detailed observational logs of how participants responded to the interventions, we were able to probe real needs and motivations by demonstrating potential everyday solutions and getting immediate feedback on their value. Within the three experimental settings, these are the interventions we made:

Acoustic intervention: We introduced a sound transformation system called Future Acoustic in the high concentration area. The system listens to background noise and reduces its distracting qualities by generating a more harmonious and pleasant replacement sound. This innovation was installed on desks to see if it would successfully reduce acoustic distraction and increase productivity and concentration.

Lighting intervention: We installed user-controllable lighting to provide workers with laptop control over the brightness and colour balance of their working environment. Participants were also able to choose from dynamic lighting programmes appropriate to their task, for example a meeting or solo task. This intervention aimed to discover the best ways of offering lighting control to office workers in relation to work activity and time of day.

Lighting intervention installed in a Japanese workspace

Technology intervention: Wireless ergonomic keyboards and mice were introduced and tested to see how well workers adapted to these new technologies and to what extent they were useful in shared office environments.

Adjustable furniture: Electronically operated height-adjustable desks were provided to enable workers to stand for periods of time during the day, as well as easily set the optimum ergonomic position for working while seated. Fully adjustable chairs were also made available to test how well workers corrected their position when using shared facilities such as hot-desking.

Alternative furniture: As an experiment, we included reading chairs designed for the care market and a sofa that reclined into a day bed in the contemplation zone. Our aim was to see how workers would react to a type of furniture offering much higher levels of comfort and adaptability, and a wider range of working positions. Would such solutions be welcomed or be seen as stigmatising?

Adjustable height desk installed in UK workplace

Natural intervention: A curtain of continuously falling water drops was added to the design installation to gauge user reaction to more natural elements in the office environment. A 'rain curtain' was installed, making a soothing sound that masked distracting noises and affected the humidity of the air, as well as acting as a space divider to shield a quiet zone.

Acoustics, lighting and technology

As we anticipated, the design interventions had a big impact. Office workers were not hesitant in trying them out and giving their views on the potential benefit. The acoustic intervention based on an intelligent reactive sound system was welcomed for the control it gave the user over what type of sound should replace general background noise – falling water or choral sounds, for example. The sound would become gradually louder in response to the increased volume of noise around it. The system was viewed as helpful in reducing acoustic distractions in open-plan space, although some participants wondered if it might also be annoying. Here is a range of opinions:

'The acoustic noise masking technology – I would love to have this in the area I work in now.'

'I found the acoustic technology helped concentration, because it made the space seem more private, I was less concerned about disturbing others.'

'It could allow you to attend a teleconference at your own desk without disturbing others.'

'Future Acoustic helped with concentration because when people came in and were talking, I was disturbed. Increasing the volume of noise, it was easier to tune the voices out.'

'It helped my concentration, but it may drive others mad! I would like more choice of sounds, perhaps water, birdsong or wind.'

'It had a peaceful, restful pace that blocked distractions by being consistent.'

An intelligent lighting system that could be controlled by the user also appealed to many research participants, who are disadvantaged by centrally controlled lighting regimes that set automatic general adjustment for the whole office. Many approved of lighting that changes with the time of day, but wanted to control this aspect themselves. Here are some representative views:

'The concept of the lighting system was very interesting – after just a few minutes in this area, I could feel the benefits compared to the lighting we have currently in the building which can be harsh sometimes.'

'I held a very personal meeting with my manager. I found the lighting relaxed me and made the meeting less stressful, I also felt more open with my manager through being relaxed. My manager also commented how less stressful the meeting was and how good the lighting was.'

'I would prefer controllable lighting in my work area, near my screen and desktop to control incoming glare from windows and lights.'

'I would value being able to turn down the lighting, though I don't want automatically changing light.'

The response to our technological intervention – namely, the introduction of wireless keyboards and mice, as well as new-style ergonomic 'wave' keyboards with a slightly different configuration to the standard keyboard – illustrated the problems with set-up that many older workers experience. Many participants could not work out how to operate these new devices, finding the process of set-up counter-intuitive. However, once shown how to turn them on, users were generally receptive to these technological innovations:

'With the keyboard and mouse, I couldn't make it work until someone came and showed me how.'

'The Wave keyboard had a better feel [than a traditional keyboard].'

Wave keyboard installed as technology intervention

Response to furniture interventions

The adjustable furniture intervention drew a mixed response. The highly ergonomic chairs we provided for optimal comfort were generally regarded as 'complicated' to adjust for personal preference. In a hot-desk scenario, where participants would take time to adjust the chair to their preferred setting only to find, should they return to that space, that the next user would have readjusted the chair, such a process was unhelpful. However, the introduction of sit-stand desks with an adjustable height function was universally welcomed. Older knowledge workers appreciated being able to change position and to stand up and work at their desk, especially in concentration or contemplation zones shielded from the general hubbub of a large open-plan office:

'The adjustable desk is perfect for this type of area.'

'The sit-stand desk was brilliant...'

'Changing the position of the desk height aided intense concentration, but it needed an adjustable stool with foot rest to give variety and choice, I would sometimes prefer to stand to work.'

As with the adjustable furniture, the alternative furniture intervention divided the crowd. Most research participants noticed that care furniture had been introduced into the work environment, and while they appreciated higher levels of comfort to aid rest and recovery in a contemplation space, they were less keen on the style. Here are some typical comments:

'The (contemplation) area is informal and welcoming. I loved the different types of chairs, and in particular the recliner.'

'The reading chairs seemed suited for small people, they needed foot rests and looked straight out of an OAP day centre!'

'The reclining sofa would be useful in a dedicated quiet zone.'

'The reading chairs were not suitable for the office, as they looked too much like something you might find in a hospital.'

Care furniture reupholstered using modern fabrics to heighten levels of comfort

Finally, what did older knowledge workers make of our 'natural' intervention? Some responded well to the idea of a 'rain curtain' creating a wall of raindrops as a space divider. They found that the noise of the rain brought a sense of calm and aided concentration. Others, however, were rather less keen. Here are those mixed reactions:

'Maybe it's my imagination but…the air felt fresher and better, the sound acted as helpful white noise.'

'The rain curtain had a subliminal impact after an initial surprise, it was relaxing. I would choose to place water features all over the place…'

'The rain curtain became a bit soporific after a while, I would not want one in my workspace.'

'The rain curtain made me feel a bit cold.'

Provocations for design change

Our six design interventions were created to deliberately exaggerate effects based on issues that participants raised during the interviews. They acted as provocations for older workers engaging with our research, prodding them to consider wider aspects of design

The Rain Curtain, a natural intervention designed by Catherine Green of the RCA Helen Hamlyn Centre

that they may find conducive to their needs. Yet one of the most important elements of this workplace experiment was that those interventions that were most acceptable to our target group were also those that were most inclusive to all ages in the workforce. Interventions that were perceived to single out for preferential treatment or stigmatise older workers – adapted care furniture, for example – proved less popular than those that had appeal for all (such as user-controlled lighting, sound-masking technology or sit-stand desks). We were therefore reinforced in our view that an inclusive approach to design can have the maximum benefit for a multigenerational workforce.

The interventions also highlighted an urgent need to rethink generic use of office space. Current mapping of the corporate work environment shows how large open-plan spaces – typically based on the low-segmentation/low-choice, one-size-fits-all model – are supplemented by a variety of breakout, meeting and social areas. However, for knowledge workers, such arrangements appear detrimental to the needs of concentration in terms of noise, distraction and lack of confidentiality while not going far enough to meet the challenge of intense collaborative tasks.

The mere facts of geographical proximity and line of sight are no substitute for a dedicated project setting designed to facilitate and enhance teamwork. A drive towards 'smarter' working with clean-desk policies and hot-desking further disadvantages those experienced employees whose contribution companies should be maximising.

While organisations address the challenges of concentration and collaboration to varying degrees depending on the individual corporate context, they appear to overlook completely the need for all workers to rest, reflect and restore in a quiet setting shielded from surveillance and supervisory control. Contemplation space represents a missing dimension of office design. This is not surprising – the provision of such space will not only require a shift in wider cultural attitude towards rest and recuperation whilst still at work, but also the emergence of new design models for a workplace typology that many employers find difficult to grasp.

Three generic types of workplace

A key conclusion of our *Welcoming Workplace* study was that organisations should redesign their environment by considering three generic types of office space for all their knowledge workers – settings for concentration, collaboration and contemplation. Central to all three spaces should be the opportunity to work in a number of different ergonomic positions – seated, standing, reclining and so on – to encourage healthier workstyles. There should also be provision of inclusively designed amenities and solutions that benefit everyone – not just ageing employees and those approaching the retirement age.

In the following chapters, we go on to describe in more detail how spaces for concentration, collaboration and contemplation might be designed. We report on the organisations that have piloted new approaches in these areas and speak to leading creative pioneers about how they generate knowledge in their own workspaces.

16 Spaces to concentrate

Getting into 'flow' depends on a dedicated design approach

The ability to concentrate is often one of the first casualties of any move to open plan by knowledge-based organisations. So when the pharmaceutical giant Novartis commissioned a pilot project in 2003 for its finance department as part of the redevelopment of its St Johann campus in Basel, Switzerland, the company was determined that achieving a more open and dynamic environment should not be to the detriment of the singular concentrated work that finance people need to do.

Designer Sevil Peach of Sevil Peach Gence Associates faced a difficult brief – to create a plan to foster greater teamwork, communication and interaction, but without forgoing first principles of privacy and quiet. The resulting scheme is a well-conceived workplace on one floor for 70 people that lets individuals and teams work in the way they want according to task. In a refurbished 1970s precast concrete building, the 1,190 sq metre space is divided into more intimate work areas. A shared workbench runs as a central

Drapes create concentration space in Novartis pilot
scheme designed by Sevil Peach Gence Associates

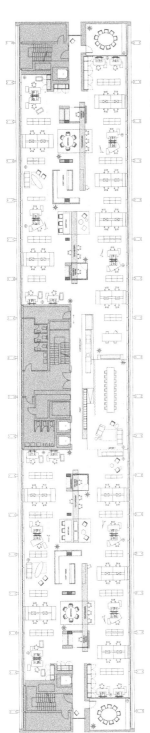

spine through the environment, allowing for breakout areas and informal meetings. At either end of the spine are enclosed cabins for concentrated work, confidential discussions or conference calls. Formal meeting and video-conferencing rooms can be found at each end of the floor. Open workstations can be personalised and the floor is adorned with artwork and photographs from the Novartis archives.

The Novartis pilot thus balances the needs to collaborate and concentrate, achieving a more open style without turning the office into one giant brainstorm room. Sevil Peach, one of Europe's leading office interior designers, believes that user involvement is essential to getting that design balance right. She says of the Novartis project: 'On the architectural level, we proposed solutions that aimed to erase the fears of employees whose vision of open-plan work environments conjured up an image of the rubber stamp approach of a sea of desks lacking privacy and personalization. We sought to create definable, defensible group spaces that allowed the individual to work within an understandable landscape, and on a familiar scale.'

Peach believes that you don't necessarily require enclosed cabins or cocoons to create good concentration space, although these can help. Simply creating a visual 'stop' in the floorplate with plants, screens, hanging textiles, low partitions or softer lighting can signal that this area of the office floor has a different protocol – one requiring quiet, with no phone calls or physical interruptions to disrupt concentrated work. 'People will self-regulate their behaviour and lower their voices if they know the rules and if they have been involved in deciding what those rules should be,' says Peach.

Lighting as a lever to concentrate

Elsewhere in Europe, knowledge-intensive companies are finding new design solutions to help their premium employees focus more effectively. Amsterdam-based Uxus Design, for example, uses lighting as a lever to aid concentration in its studio environment. Spotlights

Novartis floor plan by Sevil Peach Gence Associates

and uplighters are combined with task lights on the desk to minimise the need for high ambient light levels, so creating a softer, more comfortable ambience without compromising functionality. This is a combination many older workers requested in our research.

In addition, good use is made of natural light, using cotton drapes to diffuse the light and provide more local control. The decor is attractive without being distracting. The bench-style desking enables workers to have more space when occupancy levels permit, and its proximity to alternative settings provides the variety people need for different activities.

The Uxus Design studio in Amsterdam uses cotton drapes to dampen sound and diffuse natural light
(Photo courtesy of Mathijs Wessing)

Choosing furniture for focus

Here is another example. An open-plan office designed by Ann-Charlotte Nilsson for a Swedish IT consultancy in the centre of Stockholm creates an effective workspace for sustained concentration by considered use of furniture. There is a range of desk types to choose from according to user preference, including height-adjustable desks that allow workers to stand for periods of the day. Desks by the windows are double-spaced without partitions, so that occupants can spread out and use more space. The desks away from the windows have large whiteboards adjacent to each desk, allowing workers to work off-screen, map out their ideas and pin up charts and graphics. For older knowledge workers who resent always being forced to work out of a computer screen, this is a valuable innovation. All personal possessions are kept in large lockers in the centre of the room. Uplighting helps to create an open, airy feel to the space, making it pleasant to be in for the long periods of time that workers require to concentrate hard on the task in hand.

Modul 1 IT consultancy workplace in Stockholm addresses issues of concentration

Reaching an optimal experience

It is no surprise that we should dwell briefly here on two consultancy environments from the creative industries. Helping people to focus and get into the 'flow' of work assumes a greater priority with creative tasks. The leading psychologist Mihaly Csikszentmihalyi has written widely on 'flow' – on the 'optimal experience' of creative enjoyment and total involvement with certain types of work, and on achieving a state of consciousness so satisfying and a state of concentration so total that all surrounding distractions are completely shut out. As part of his research, Csikszentmihalyi interviewed many creative individuals about their work. Some common themes emerged. The poet Mark Strand told him: 'You're right in the work. You lose your sense of time, you're completely enraptured, you're completely caught up in what you're doing…there's no future or past, it's just an extended present in which you're making meaning.'

As part of the same study, the cell biologist Joseph G Gall explained: 'To go into a dark room and look through the microscope and see these glowing objects…It's just beautiful. I can sit in front of a microscope for three or four hours at a time, just looking at the material and analysing it…This can be very disconcerting to other people in the degree to which I can concentrate on something and not pay to much attention to what's going on around me.' A composer told Csikszentmihalyi: 'You're in an ecstatic state to such a point that you feel as though you almost don't exist. I have experienced this time and again. My hand seems devoid of myself, and I have nothing to do with what's happening. I just sit there watching it in a state of aware and wonderment. And (the music) just flows out of itself.'

From his research, Csikszentmihalyi deduced that a state of flow is achieved when we feel a number of things: we are completely involved in what we are doing – focused, concentrated; we experience a sense of ecstasy – of being outside everyday reality; we feel great inner clarity – of knowing what needs to be done and how well we are doing; we accept that the act is doable and that our skills are adequate to the task; we feel a sense of serenity with no worries about oneself, and of timelessness – thoroughly focused on the present, hours seem to pass like minutes, Finally, there is intrinsic motivation – whatever produces flow becomes its own reward.

Csikszentmihalyi believes that it is the relationship between the scale of the challenge and the ability of the individual to meet that challenge that unlocks the 'optimal experience' of flow. When the challenge is great but the skill level is much lower, the result is anxiety. When the opposite is true, the result is apathy. When a high level of challenge meets a high level of ability to meet that challenge, then flow can be achieved. How often have we been unable to reach optimum concentration because we have been distracted from a major challenge, perhaps due to our environment, and therefore we are creatively aroused but not in flow? How often have we missed out because we have all the skills to meet a challenge that is not quite worthy of our total attention, and we are therefore in cruise control but not in flow?

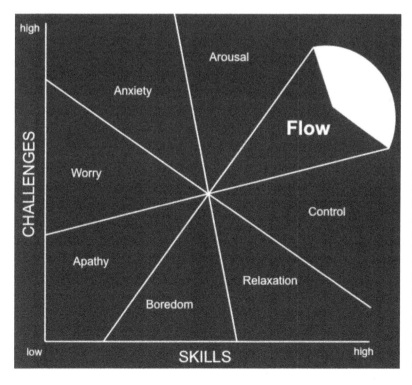

Chart showing the Flow concept by Mihaly Csikszentmihalyi as a relationship between challenge and skill (Source: Mihaly Csikszentmihalyi Phd. Quality of Life Research Centre, Claremont Graduate University, Claremont CA)

Workspace design and the state of flow

It is not hard to see why the workplace design community has latched onto the ideas of Mihaly Csikszentmihalyi about 'flow'. Csikszentmihalyi's studies have shown that the more time an individual spends in flow during the working week, the better the overall quality of their reported experience. People who are more frequently in flow are especially likely to feel 'strong', 'active', 'creative', 'concentrated' or 'motivated'. These feelings are prized assets for employers – in a knowledge-based economy where creative work is increasingly relied upon to add value and where the most experienced people might contemplate leaving the workforce altogether, ensuring that senior professionals can achieve total focus must therefore be a first base for office design.

However design practitioners are often diverted by the rival demands of teamwork and collaboration in designing work environments. Finding the headspace for concentrated work requires not just the provision of physical privacy (booths, cabins, caves, screened-off areas and so on) but also psychological privacy, as design researcher Tim Parsons recognised when he undertook a study at the Royal College of Art, London, in 2001 entitled *Headspace: Privacy in Open Plan Offices*. Through a series of observations in bustling media offices, Parsons discovered that territorial and physical elements to aid concentration and privacy tend to be ineffective and irrelevant if the mind is unsettled and unfocused on the job in hand.

Parsons created a series of experiments to give people greater psychological privacy without the need to build walls and create private enclaves. Aware that martial artists can perform rituals in close physical proximity as part of a large group and yet remain highly focused on the movements of their own bodies, Parsons speculated whether office workers could get into flow despite all the bustle and noise around them. He created a series of cultural artefacts to suggest the idea of greater privacy without actually giving workers any more personal space.

Umbrella chair created by Tim Parsons (RCA, 2001) and tested in situ with office workers

An 'umbrella chair' featured an umbrella in the backrest that could be opened to provide an acoustic shield and act as a sign saying 'do not disturb me'. A 'no door mat' was introduced to give open-plan occupants an opportunity to delineate their personal threshold that should not be crossed (the door plays a central role in cellular office culture). A 'desk postbox' was positioned on the edge of a worker's personal domain to avoid mail and document deliveries from colleagues interrupting the flow of concentration; after all, the postman does not stride right into your living room and chuck all the mail on to your living room table, but that is broadly what happens with the office mail and your workstation.

When Parsons tested these 'permeable privacy' artefacts, the results revealed a lack of cultural rituals that can protect concentration and focus within open-plan space. One can conclude from this that it is not so much the openness of the space *per se* that is at fault, but the tendency of such environments to exacerbate feelings of loss of personal control (such as constant interruptions, mail dropped into your lap and so on) that do so much to impede reaching a state of flow. People simply do not understand what might be expected of them in open environments and what the norms of behaviour should be.

Understanding our place in the process

In creative workplaces where the rules are well understood and people clearly understand their role in the scheme of things, it is perfectly possible to focus hard in an entirely open studio. Betty Jackson is one of Britain's best-known fashion designers, with special collections for high street names Marks & Spencer and Debenhams. Early in her career she worked as chief designer at the fashion collective Quorum alongside design legends Ossie Clark and Celia Birtwell before launching her own company in 1981, with her husband and business partner David Cohen.

Betty Jackson photographed in her London studio

Betty Jackson told us: 'My studio is completely open – we're a very democratic company. I am sitting here looking at pattern cutters, at seamstresses and at fabrics. It's nice to see other people. I can't see the point of going into a room and just seeing people's backs. Working facing the wall or looking into a computer is not how it should be. We have another room in which to be silent – anyone can use it.'

For Betty Jackson: 'The most important thing for me in terms of having a creative workspace is daylight. My studio is very light and I can see the sky. That matters a great deal.' The way she describes her working environment does not conjure up a strictly regimented place ('we collect a lot of stuff here, it's lovely but it creeps up and then we need a huge clear-out') but it is clearly one in which there are protocols in place to enable creative focus on the act of designing fashion clothing. Betty Jackson and her team can get into flow and they derive great personal satisfaction from the work.

Principles of space for concentration

Spaces to concentrate do not need to be bricked off from the main office. People requiring some quiet and privacy should not be required to climb inside a small cabin or cave, or to abandon the office entirely and take the work home. Our research suggests that progressive organisations can take a number of simple, relatively inexpensive steps to provide spaces for older knowledge workers to undertake tasks that require sustained focus, high levels of analysis and attention to detail or privacy.

First, it must be recognised by senior management that such spaces are not just necessary but absolutely essential and that there are different options to create these areas – as separate rooms, special booths or as designated areas of the main office, screened off from other areas. These concentration spaces should be separated from the noise and distraction of the general office and governed by strict protocols for working (for example, no mobile phone calls or loud conversations, as in a library).

Special consideration should be given to the needs of mobile, part-time or 'drop-in' workers (many older employees fall into these categories) and indeed anyone who wants to get away from their normal environment to complete a particularly demanding task. These spaces should be located away from noisy facilities such as kitchens and cafés, print-rooms or social spaces. They should be equipped with different types of furniture and adjustable settings to allow for a range of working positions, as poor ergonomics and uncomfortable posture will adversely affect the ability to get into flow. Where budgets allow, height-adjustable desks can facilitate standing for periods of the day – a healthy approach to working.

We advise that, where possible, window views should be available in these spaces to connect people to the outside world, as this is an aid to concentration (completely enclosed, unconnected spaces are difficult to focus in for any length of time). Natural light should be brought into play wherever possible, with fabric curtains and blinds introduced to diffuse light. Artificial lighting schemes should provide task lights at the desk – an important consideration for ageing eyes and for reading printouts off-screen – and a lower and more pleasant level of general ambient lighting within the concentration space.

Finally, designers should consider the use of audio-masking technology and sound transformation systems that can reduce distracting noise, as well as more traditional baffles and fabrics that absorb sound. Remember that in every study of the modern office environment, noise is the main bugbear. Concentrated work demands that we turn down the volume.

① An intelligent audio-masking system listens to background noise and creates harmonious sounds instead.

② Motorised height-adjustable desk allows users to stand for periods of the day. Effective for easily and quickly adapting to different ergonomic needs.

③ Task lights are important for ageing eyes, and off screen work, but they also allow for lower and more pleasant ambient light.

④ Window views should be democratically available to connect people to the outside world. Users should be able to diffuse natural light with curtains.

Design guidance on spaces for concentration
(Welcoming Workplace, 2008)

17   Spaces to collaborate

The convenience of geographical proximity is never enough

When global communication giant Nokia decided to relocate 80 of its UK-based designers from the rural backwater of Farnborough in Hampshire to a new creative hub in the centre of London, space to collaborate was central to the move. Nokia wanted to re-energise its existing design team and attract fresh talent with a brand new home in Soho that prioritised teamworking and social interaction.

Linda Morey Smith of designers MoreySmith led the revamp of three floors of a building in London's Great Pulteney Street to create Nokia's 35,000 sq ft London design studio. Fundamental to the scheme are its communal areas: a workshop room, breakout areas and live project rooms providing space conducive to group work. The centrally located project rooms enable teams of designers to work away from their open-plan desks in spaces dedicated to collaboration. These functional workspaces are equipped with moveable furniture and controllable lighting. Two giant revolving acrylic panels separate the communal areas from a presentation room. White space creates a neutral blank canvas on which project teams create.

Nokia's London design studio by MoreySmith
(Photo courtesy of Alistair Little)

Planning for teamwork

Linda Morey Smith, who has also designed offices for Nokia design teams in Helsinki and Copenhagen, believes collaboration spaces need to be deliberately planned: 'It is all about being seen to collaborate, about promoting movement and buzz within the office. It is not enough just to sit people next to each other in basic open plan and hope that intense project work will simply happen. You have to provide the right settings with the right tools so that people can work together properly. It is much more than just about geographical proximity.' Nokia's Mark Mason, who worked on the relocation from the client side, agrees: 'We set ourselves the goal of creating an environment which *fosters* collaboration.'

While Nokia's design team is predominantly young, the engineering workforce at the nearby London Fitzrovia office of engineers Arup – also designed by MoreySmith – is much older on average. However similar principles to encourage interaction and teamwork are evident in a scheme for 400 staff, which has a flexible communal hub at its heart complete with breakout areas, café and feature staircase. Within open-plan areas, coloured bespoke acrylic screens feature magnetic displays and provide writing surfaces, informally dividing space and combining with mobile team tables in flexible layouts to create versatile collaboration space to suit any project requirement. 'Companies are now very keen on briefing office designers to create project space, especially in knowledge industries like professional services,' says Linda Morey Smith. 'They don't leave it to chance.'

Reaping dividends from project space

Public relations agency Edelman exemplifies that attitude. When the company moved its 260 staff to a new 38,000 sq ft space on a single floor in London's Victoria district, the office scheme created by architectural firm Gensler was all about improving collaboration and teamwork. Space in the Edelman office is flexible, allowing for variable density. A few directors' offices double as meeting rooms. Conference rooms expand and contract to accommodate a constant flow of meetings and events. When people need to collaborate, dedicated space is made available. There is also an impressive line-up of social areas.

Architect Gensler's collaboration space for public relations agency Edelman

Edelman's CEO Robert Phillips, who led his company into the new environment, has claimed that the radical shift in working practice paid dividends within a year of moving into the new space. Staff turnover decreased by 20 per cent and the number of sick days also went down. The win rate on pitches went up and so did levels of staff satisfaction – by a meteoric 60 per cent according to Edelman's employee survey.

Creating innovation hubs

Edelman's work in fast-moving industry sectors dictated its need to promote teamwork to react swiftly and reconfigure constantly. Large corporate organisations face similar challenges but find it harder to be nimble on their feet due to reasons of scale and bureaucracy. There are ways round the problem, however. GlaxoSmithKline Consumer Healthcare, for example, worked with architects and consultants DEGW to create a series of innovation hubs at the company's facilities in Parsippany, New Jersey, and Weybridge in the UK. These hubs – the result of a scheme called Project Ignite – provide dedicated teams with space for collaboration. In the words of one seasoned R&D leader at GlaxoSmithKline, 'We're overloaded with information in our environment and the hubs are like the good old days when people talked to each other. They're a bit retro.'

Two key elements are central to the approach. Each team is given its own high-quality project room to spread out, use as they wish and determine their own protocols for ways of working. The walls of the room form a continuous project space, enabling the group to visually pin up and track ideas. The second feature is the use of open 'kitchen tables' in the centre of the hub. These 'kitchen tables' break down communication barriers and enable impromptu meetings and reviews to take place, adding to the overall objectives of the hub project space. Consumer rooms (which bring consumer research to life) and sensory areas (which animate the results of lab testing and evaluation) are additions to the interdisciplinary mix.

Working on the grounds that 'you can't improve it if you can't measure it', DEGW surveyed team performance once the hubs were put in place and recorded a dramatic impact on business performance. GlaxoSmithKline employees reported that they made decisions more speedily, wasted less time during the working day (40 minutes per person on average), were more responsive to market needs, felt more innovative as a group and generally felt happier in the workplace.

Breaking down departmental silos

Project Ignite pulled entire teams of knowledge workers out of highly-cellular, owned accommodation into more open, unassigned space. But it did not simply abandon these premium employees in low-choice, low-segmentation, one-size-fits-all open plan. It

Innovation hub developed by architects DEGW for GlaxoSmithKline in Weybridge, UK (Photos courtesy of Chris Gascoigne)

thought carefully about how it wanted its teams of scientists, marketers and salespeople to collaborate in teams. It supported the cultural shift with a change management programme that developed the protocols to underpin such a radical move. Focus group sessions allowed staff members to arrive at a consensus on how the innovation hubs should function.

Underpinning the entire exercise was the conviction that the redesign of the environment should be driven by the requirements of global brands rather than professional disciplines, so removing departmental silos. And given the nature of the business, there was a focus on brand immersion in the innovation hubs – special solutions were developed for merchandising, lighting, graphic imagery and audio-visual display.

Other multinationals have done similar things. Pharmaceutical company Pfizer, which makes Viagra, took the opportunity of a move to a leafy new campus at Walton Oaks, Surrey, UK, to introduce project space for cross-functional teams. The scheme was designed by architect Sheppard Robson. According Maria Hazard, Pfizer's Property and Procurement Manager, 'We used the relocation to change the way we work, to build better communication and better teamworking. Now medics, marketers and finance people are all co-located.' Like the GlaxoSmithKline innovation hubs, a cultural change management programme at Pfizer established consensus on the protocols around such things as project meetings and shared printing services.

Pfizer's leafy campus in Walton Oaks Surrey by Sheppard Robson was designed to improve team work

Building a meeting 'tree'

While the project areas in some companies today look fairly conventional in planning – Pfizer's green, award-winning headquarters at Walton Oaks lies low in the landscape with five office 'fingers' radiating off a curved central spine to offer teams green and pleasant exterior views – other organisations are conceiving of more radical ways to create spaces for collaboration.

In Sydney, financial services giant Macquarie has worked with designer Clive Wilkinson to create a major new development at One Shelley Street for 3,000 staff. The futuristic scheme features a 'meeting tree' that grows upwards within the envelope of the building. Instead of a horizontal suite of project or meeting spaces enclosed on one floor, the idea of collaboration permeates the entire organisation from top to bottom. Wilkinson's initial

concept for the project was to have a series of moveable meeting rooms on giant cranes like shipping containers. When that idea proved difficult to achieve, the meeting tree took shape. 'It's a business transformation project rather than a real estate project,' Wilkinson told us. The new Macquarie headquarters opened in autumn 2009.

The giant whiteboard

Where the workplace is freed from the dictates of an owner-occupier, the space for teamwork can become even more exaggerated by design. Momentum is an innovation centre on a Danish science park for use by businesses and public institutions. It was unconventionally designed by artists Bosch & Fjord as a dedicated environment for teamwork, its project space maximising flexibility for group interactions.

The walls of Momentum's project rooms are a giant whiteboard, allowing projects to be planned, brainstormed and documented. The furniture is free to follow the drawing, and can

Concept sketch for Macquarie headquarters, Sydney, Australia: collaborative space permeates through the building. Clive Wilkinson Architects. (Original sketch by architect Clive Wilkinson)

Danish innovation centre Momentum designed by Bosch & Fjord (Photo courtesy of Elsje van Ree)

be easily reconfigured to suit a range of activities from large meetings to small-group and individual work. Even the lighting can be manipulated by hand to address different activities. The elements introduced by Bosch & Fjord at Momentum illustrate the differences between a dedicated project space and a traditional meeting room and they can be adapted to corporate office use with relative ease.

Like innovation centres, serviced offices are also getting smarter about facilitating collaboration. Designer Sevil Peach has converted a former social security building on Amsterdam's Herengracht into a lively serviced office centre for start-up businesses. On the ground floor there is a communal area with an eclectic mix of informal meeting spaces, giving a social hub to a building type that is normally transient, anonymous and drearily corporate.

Collaboration hub: serviced office centre in Amsterdam designed by Sevil Peach

Project rooms promoted

While innovation centres, serviced offices and the like represent one place to look for the leading edge in collaboration space, innovation consultancies are another. IDEO is one of the best-known names in this area, a design-led consulting firm founded in Silicon Valley in 1991 that is independently ranked by business leaders as one of the most innovative organisations in the world. The company today has a string of nine design offices across North America, Europe and Asia. We spoke to co-founder Bill Moggridge about how IDEO organises its spaces for collaboration. Moggridge brings a formidable track record in design and innovation to the subject – he designed the world's first laptop computer and pioneered the discipline of interaction design.

Moggridge is emphatic that companies should provide dedicated areas for collaboration: 'More complicated challenges, like those we address at IDEO, demand a project space. We have dedicated more of our overall footprint to project rooms by shrinking personal space and removing individual offices.' These project rooms are dubbed 'The Shared Mind' and are at the heart of how IDEO works. 'Everything about a specific project can be found in the project room, so that when you walk in there is the sense of remembering everything instantaneously. It's a trigger for collaboration,' explains Moggridge. 'Our project rooms tend to look chaotic, with large, lightweight foamcore boards measuring 8ft x 4ft leaned against the walls. These contain all the photographs, images and post-it notes relevant to the project. Prototypes and models also lie around the place.'

Project spaces at international consulting firm IDEO are termed 'The Shared Mind'
(Photos courtesy of Nicolas Zurcher/IDEO)

Moggridge explains that individual concentrated work is done outside the project room, at a bench nearby or maybe out of the IDEO building altogether. 'At IDEO you come to work to collaborate on projects,' he says. 'If you feel you need to come in just to work on your own, then there's a problem. Being in sunny California, we tend to use the outside a lot so we work next to a fountain or lunch in the park. Flexibility is very important. Our environments team at IDEO is forever changing things: one week it's the parking lot, the next week there's artificial grass and chairs.'

Does brainstorming really work?

IDEO was originally formed so that designers, engineers and human factors experts could work together more effectively on product development, and it is widely credited with inventing many of the rituals of creative brainstorming at the 'fuzzy front end' of the innovation process. It has strict rules on listening to others, on not dismissing ideas outright however crazy they might sound and on making crude, early prototypes to test ideas. Its collaboration spaces support these principles.

Management guru Tom Peters wrote in *Forbes* magazine: 'IDEO is a zoo…experts of all flavours co-mingle in "offices" that look like cacophonous kindergarten classrooms. Brainstorming sessions, pitting a dozen minds from different disciplines against one another in raucous pursuit of zany ideas, are called on at a moment's notice.' Peters added that of all the companies he'd ever looked at or written about, 'IDEO is the only one where I'd love to work.'

Not everyone believes that brainstorming of this type actually works. Designer and engineer James Dyson is one of Britain's most successful entrepreneurs. He has created a series of market innovations and is best known for the Dyson Dual Cyclone vacuum cleaner, a worldwide bestseller that has made his company a global leader. Speaking from his R&D headquarters in Wiltshire, UK, he told us: 'At Dyson, we don't run formal brainstorming sessions. They don't work. A small group, four people at most, simply watching things being tested and how they perform – that's where the creative breakthroughs come from.'

Making open plan work for innovation

James Dyson is on record as crediting the design of his work environment as essential to the company's ascent to the business summit in the ultra-competitive world of domestic appliances. Dyson now outsells Hoover in the USA. He wrote in his 1997 autobiography *Against The Odds*: 'The offices are open plan so that everyone can communicate and feels part of the same team. The graphics and engineering people are in the centre of the office…there are no department boundaries or borders or walls, fences, ditches,

Designer at Dyson tests a prototype

Inside the Dyson's open plan development space: freedom of movement is encouraged

moats, ha-has or minefields: freedom of movement and of expression is total. I hope in this way to make everyone design conscious, and to feel encouraged to make creative contributions.'

Twelve years on, James Dyson told us that his company has kept to its philosophy of being truly open plan and geared to collaboration at its British R&D centre in Malmesbury. 'There is nothing higher than three feet. Only our lawyers have their own enclosed offices, albeit glass ones,' explains Dyson. 'What you see when you visit our R&D area is a vast cathedral space in which we have placed the workshops and testing equipment right next to where the engineers and graphic designers are creating things.'

Many companies make their corporate labs closed, inflexible, confidential places cloaked in heavy security and secrecy. Dyson takes a different view. Once you've penetrated the company's inner sanctum of innovation, there is no confidentiality and complete freedom of movement. 'You could argue that this is a bad thing, but it's also a good thing because people can vicariously take part in projects they are not formally involved in, have an idea and make a contribution.' Dyson adds: 'People are standing around testing prototypes, exploring phenomena, trying to understand how things work. They're not desk bound, they can jump around, make suggestions and tap into the enthusiasm and energy of those around them. That's why we don't run formal brainstorming sessions.'

Dyson's creative methods have served his enterprise well. He no longer welds his own team tables like he did every time his workforce grew by ten in the early pioneering days of his manufacturing company, which was formed in 1993. Today the Dyson brand has a large production base in Malaysia and a truly global reach. But he has stayed true to key tenets around teamwork, ensuring that his designers and engineers have the right space and equipment to hand to work things through.

Missing the point on teamwork

However, for every Dyson or IDEO, there are many thousands of companies out there who simply do not pay sufficient attention to designing for the chemistry of collaboration. Walls may have been torn down and offices made more open, but little has been provided that deliberately supports communication and teamwork. Co-locating workers in standard open-plan formats is not an automatic trigger for collaboration. Walking through densely occupied open offices, we have often observed people wearing headphones and sending e-mails to colleagues just a few feet from their desk.

When the *Financial Times* columnist Michael Skapinker wrote a piece entitled 'Time to be honest about open-plan offices', his rant about enhanced communication being wiped out by a loss of productivity attracted a lot of response. Skapinker's point was that all the business talk about open-plan space fostering collaboration masked the real reason companies chose to reduce cellular accommodation – cost. You can simply fit more people in. Open-plan buildings are also cheaper to heat and cooler, making them greener.

'We do not need academic studies to tell us people get less done when they have to listen to their neighbours' conversations and telephone calls,' Skapinker told his readers. Perhaps so, but academic studies like our own explain how dedicated collaboration space can be achieved. Nobody disputes the importance of teamwork to organisational success but most offices lack project spaces in which teams can communicate their ideas and work freely without worrying about making a noise, a mess or pinning things up.

Principles of space for collaboration

We advocate the provision of studio-like project or collaboration space within the work environment where people can spread out their sheets and data, talk, argue and not worry about confidentiality or tidying away before the project is completed. It is a space that can adopt a character for a period of time – it is not anonymous like most meeting rooms. This type of space should be able to be reserved by the day, week or month, and should be well-equipped with large surfaces, white boards, paper, pens, digital image capturing and audio-visual equipment – there should be a mix of digital and traditional display media. It is not a precious space – but it is private and secure for the user while it is booked, or for the duration of the project.

Space for collaboration should provide moveable furniture and flexible work settings for personalised use by individuals as well as by project teams. Bigger desks to spread things out and bigger backdrops to pin things up will enhance collaborative modes of working. Finally, lighting should be dynamic and adjustable to suit the particular task and time of day. The art of collaboration often depends on lighting to deliver the right mood and ambience within the space. The success of some of the world's innovative companies shines a light on better ways to encourage teamwork in your organisation.

① The project space is 'owned' by a team that can use it on an improptu basis, giving the team members a permanent 'hub'.

② An abundance of digital and traditional display media allows work to remain on show for long periods of time.

③ Moveable furniture and bench-style tables allow teams to congregate and individuals to spread out for solo work.

④ Dynamic lighting allows users to adjust the light to the task at hand and their specific ergonomic needs.

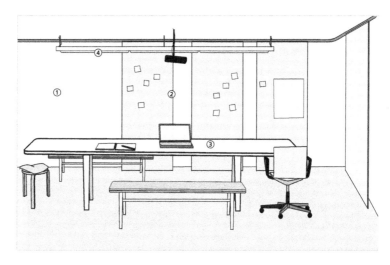

Design guidance on spaces for collaboration
(Welcoming Workplace, 2008)

18 Spaces to contemplate

Is resting the mind and body a culture change too far?

The Zurich office of Google is one of Europe's most unconventional and imaginative workplaces. Designed for up to 800 staff on seven floors of a contemporary Swiss building by architects Camenzind Evolution, the project pushes office design in many new directions. There are fire poles and spiral slides to aid 'fast connections' between floors, igloo-style cabins for team meetings complete with penguins sitting in a snowscape, an antique-themed library for quiet work and a games room for fun – facilities tailored for and designed in partnership with the overwhelmingly young Google workforce.

Contemplation space at Google Zurich by architects Camenzind Evolution based on aquarium water lounge concept

Most surprising of all is an 'acquarium water lounge' for relaxation that allows tired staff to rest fully-clothed inside a bathtub and contemplate the gentle and soothing movement of fish swimming in a series of tanks. It is a stunning and popular feature and shows the value of contemplation space for all ages – a workplace setting that is shielded from managerial surveillance, that is quiet and about letting your mind go free. The Google Zurich demographic is not typical of many of the corporate organisations we studied, but the company's willingness to provide space for rest and contemplation as well as concentration and collaboration is certainly inclusive and points the way forward.

The 1,200 sq ft Google Zurich scheme, completed in March 2008, was a textbook case of co-design with users, entailing a psychological survey, a series of one-to-one interviews and the formation of a steering committee to oversee the design work. According to architect Stefan Camenzind, it was a case of 'Don't ask people what they want – find out who they are.'

Google's Director of Global Real Estate, Chris Coleman, says the company has developed some key principles in making Googlers (or Zooglers as they are known in Zurich) productive. According to Coleman, it is important to design locally to reflect the culture of the city you are in, to create communal diversity, and to allow users to customise their own space with creative low-budget elements. An inclusive design process is not only cost efficient but also true to Google's spirit. Coleman told us: 'We have a mainly young workforce but as the company grows we have more boomers coming in to stiffen up the senior management.'

When breakout means a break

What Google has achieved in Zurich is a way to allow its employees to rest and recuperate during the working day that is true to the culture and style of a fast-moving organisation. The issue of allowing a switch-off from work during salaried hours is perhaps the sharpest design nettle of all for employers to grasp. When the first big wave of breakout and soft seat areas came into the corporate workplace in the late 1990s, the concept of breakout meant exactly that – a break from work. For older workers suffering in uniformly demanding and tiring environments, such an amenity was particularly welcome.

Very quickly, however, the introduction of wireless networks meant that breakout areas could become productive spaces again. Workers were encouraged to take their laptops into alternative seating areas and hold impromptu meetings and work sessions. Critically, these breakout spaces were in full public gaze of the rest of the open office. Often they were chosen for the views they commanded, up on a mezzanine or gallery, or positioned on a strategic corner of a circulation route.

The contemplation setting, however, reinstates the idea of breakout space in its original form – it is a place for the individual to relax and unwind, to concentrate only if they wish to do so. But it introduces a new semi-private aspect: it is free from supervisory control, a more satisfactory alternative to visiting the sick room for a lie down even if you are not feeling ill, only a bit tired. It can also incorporate natural and therapeutic elements within the design.

Taking cues from domestic space

How the contemplation setting is creatively interpreted in a workplace design scheme is up for grabs. Leading European fashion brand Mexx International, for example, worked with designer Sevil Peach of Sevil Peach Gence Associates to create distinctive contemplation space on the third floor of its Amsterdam design centre. This space has furniture that places a high value on rest and on thinking, and it is set within a boundary that provides semi-privacy; you can be in the space without feeling on show, while people outside can see whether the space is occupied without disturbing the occupants. The inclusion of hedges and grass, albeit expressed within a strictly geometric modern style, introduces an element of the outside to the space, especially under the large glass ceiling. The inclusion of domestic floor lamps further helps to create a more intimate, domesticated setting for relaxation and recuperation.

Contemplation space at Mexx International, Amsterdam creates a semi-private 'garden' zone
(Photo courtesy of Sevil Peach Gence Associates)

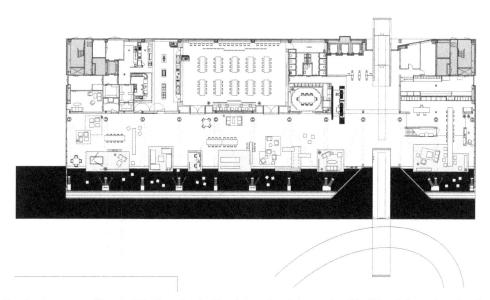

Breakout spaces positioned within floor plan for Mexx International Amsterdam (Sevil Peach Gence Associates)

Mexx International's scheme illustrates Sevil Peach's philosophy about what she describes as 'a retreat zone'. Peach believes that demographic change is much less on the radar of employers than the need to design for knowledge interactions. As a result she accepts that she must spend time convincing clients that 'shielded escape areas' must be part of the repertoire of workplace settings for a changing workforce. 'Why do we like to work from home?' she muses. 'We can open windows, wander in the garden, get coffee when we want it, work on the kitchen table and then plonk down on a sofa. We can switch behaviours. The workplace should feel like that too.'

Not surprisingly, many contemplation settings take their visual cues from domestic space. The work of Japanese architects Kazuyo Sejima and Ryue Nishizawa has influenced many workplace designers. In Nishizawa's House A in Tokyo we found many of the qualities that we propose for contemplation spaces in offices. This is not so surprising in that a contemplation space should be a break from the corporate open plan, and provide elements of domesticity. The low-tech space in House A incorporates furniture for recuperation and relaxation, natural green elements to instil calm, and an open environment to inspire deep thought.

At the Momentum innovation centre in Denmark that we discussed in relation to collaboration in the previous chapter, there is a contemplation zone designed by Bosch and Fjord that mimics a domestic garden pond with a wooden stepped terrace leading down to a small internal lake.

Green retreat space designed by
Japanese architect Ryue Nishizawa
(Photo courtesy of Office of Ryue
Nishizawa)

Bosch & Fjord's contemplation zone
at Momentum, Denmark
(Photo courtesy of Else van Ree)

Allowing creativity to flourish

The quality of a contemplative environment is what marks out a favourite workspace
for many creative people. Such space is often domestic in feel or in reality. Sir Terence
Conran is one of the world's best-known designers, restaurateurs and retailers. The
founder of the Habitat chain and patron of the Design Museum told us: 'I do my best
creative work sitting at a table in the garden in the sunshine with a bottle of wine and a
cigar and a large pad of cheap detail paper and a 3B pencil. That's when it really works
for me. I use seashore pebbles to hold the papers down, otherwise the paper blows all
over the flowerbeds. I retire to my greenhouse during the winter.' It is a powerfully
evocative image.

Fashion pioneer Wayne Hemingway founded the acclaimed Red or Dead clothing label with his wife Gerardine before focusing on affordable and social design, including housing, as the head of Hemingway Design. He works at home in Sussex one day a week from a large teepee in the garden. The London office of his design firm is a ramshackle, suburban, seven-bed house in north London, which he converted on a residential street.

'The whole domestic feel works for the company,' Hemingway told us. 'When people visit us, it turns their expectations inside out. There are no signs in the hall or on the outside that this is a design studio, not a house. The most important attribute in a creative workspace is happiness. It's all about making our people feel comfortable and happy. We have 20 staff working here. Our boardroom table is a big kitchen table with hotplates built in, so you can cook vegetables during meetings. We grow our own fruit and veg in the garden. We're so glad we chose this quirky route.'

Sir Terence Conran pictured in his garden

Making people happier

Wayne Hemingway's message is that quality of life really matters at work. A contented team is more likely to be productive and loyal, and what creates happiness at work is changing gear and doing those quasi-domestic, stress-relieving things such as making a cup of coffee or a light meal or putting your

Wayne Hemmingway pictured in his teepee workspace in Sussex. (Photo courtesy of Hemingway Design)

feet up that the modern scientifically managed workplace has done so much to crush out of existence.

If people want to lie down for half an hour to recharge the batteries, why not let them? It makes evident sense but many companies refuse to accept that a strong work ethic can embrace such a notion, and cannot contemplate such a shift in culture. For an ageing workforce, the unrelenting image of the office as a machine for working in without escape or space to think can become torture, especially for those who see retirement receding into the distance with the pensions crisis.

Some years ago, we participated in a project called *Kinder* at the Royal College of Art between the designer Pascal Anson and a Swedish furniture company. Anson designed a series of workstation objects to improve life for the sedentary office worker at an intermediate scale – larger than desktop products but smaller than furniture. One of the objects was a 'mini-garden', a natural fence between neighbours who would jointly tend the greenery. Another was a 'mini-bed' so that employees could rest their head on the desk in a comfortable position and take 40 winks. The mini-bed idea was viewed by the industry partner as ideal for Scandinavian companies but unacceptable for UK or American markets. Their reaction told us everything we needed to know about the unbending Anglo-Saxon attitude to taking rest and recuperation at work. This is the culture that will need to change if older knowledge workers are to get the work settings they really deserve.

Mini bed tested in busy office as part of Kinder project by Pascal Anson (RCA, 2001)

Principles of space for contemplation

We believe it is important that contemplation spaces are provided that give people of all ages in the workforce somewhere to recuperate from the stress and noise of the normal working environment; a place to go when workers are tired, or need to prepare for an energetic task; somewhere they can relax, create new ideas or simply do nothing. A contemplation space should provide a calm, inclusive environment free from distraction and surveillance. We envisage it as a non-bookable area, with a variety of adjustable furniture, where people can go for periods of ten minutes to several hours.

It is a space that the office community respects, within which workers can expect not to be interrupted and people will not make phone calls or have loud conversations. It may have strong natural and organic elements, rich with plants, water, fabric banners and adjustable lighting, giving it a different feel to the office atmosphere elsewhere. There are many different ways a space for contemplation can be designed. The common denominator, however, is that it should be quiet and enclosed, with a degree of privacy. It carries elements of a comfortable domestic environment.

Just as modern working life has meant that the home has begun to accommodate work, so contemplation space redresses the balance by becoming a 'home' within the office. It is not a sick bay, though, and needs to avoid the stigma of illness, so that staff members of all ages and abilities feel they can use the space freely. This is particularly important considering workers' long exposure to computer screens and mobile devices. Migraines, stress and sore eyes should no longer force workers to take the day off, but should be catered for on-site in a supportive way. Providing sensitively planned space for contemplation is a way to achieve this.

① An 'office garden' provides for informal interactions, a sense of ownership over the environment, and an organic element to the office.

② A variety of furniture, including a day bed, and ergonomically supportive reading chairs allow people to recuperate and think.

③ A curtain of falling water provides a sense of acoustic peace, humidifies the air, and adds elements of purity and nature to the space.

④ This area is semi-private, not on show but not hidden away. These semi-transparent dividers help to create the right levels of privacy.

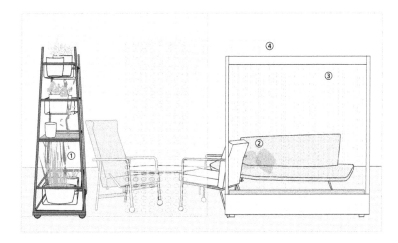

Design guidance on spaces for contemplation
(Welcoming Workplace, 2008)

19 Making it happen

A mix of knowledge settings is what really matters

In discussing dedicated settings for concentration, collaboration and contemplation, as we have done in the previous three chapters, it is tempting to see each typology as an end in itself. However it is important to point out that the different spaces for knowledge work are not mutually exclusive, that they are a means to enhance knowledge work in its totality, and that it is the interrelationship between them that creates the very best places to work.

The Novartis office in Basel that we singled out for its approach to concentration also does collaboration very well. The London Nokia studio has exceptional teamwork spaces but it does not neglect quiet work. Google's Zurich workplace may offer a water lounge for contemplation and recuperation, but its privacy and collaboration facilities are also designed with great flair. There is even a massage room at Google to encourage the healthier workstyle.

A range of settings

Progressive employers take an intelligent, multifaceted approach to the demands of knowledge work by providing a range of different settings for different types of work, all within the same workplace scheme and sometimes achieved by doing different things with the same large open-plan space. The Dutch insurance company Interpolis exemplifies this attitude to providing choice in where to work depending on the task at hand. Its Tilburg headquarters designed by Veldhoen + Co interprets the words 'inter' and 'polis' through a network of interior structures, squares and neighbourhoods linked by pathways.

At Interpolis, an enclosed artist-inspired space provides an enclosed setting for private, concentrated work; a bright meeting area on illuminated tiles is a dedicated space for collaboration; and a grouping of giant winged chairs designed by Jurgen Bey help to create

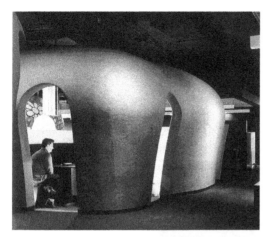

Spaces to concentrate, collaborate and contemplate at Interpolis Tilberg, The Netherlands (Veldhoen + Co)
(Photos courtesy of Jean Simons)

a space for contemplation and recuperation. Throughout the world of workplace design more examples like Interpolis, which was completed in 2003, are beginning to emerge.

Addressing the key issues

Indeed we can sense the tectonic plates moving under the issue of extended working lives in the knowledge economy. In autumn 2009, the UK Government published a major report, *Building a Society for All Ages*, in which it stated its intention to review the default retirement age of 65 and its determination to use inclusive design as a tool to create the products, services and spaces to help individuals to work longer. Evidence from our *Welcoming Workplace* study was submitted the report's authors.

At the same time, Austrian manufacturer Bene launched what it claimed to be the first modular furniture system for knowledge workers. Designed by London consultants Pearson Lloyd and taking its inspiration from sources as diverse as the Parisian café, the West African Toguna, the Spanish Steps in Rome and the Giants Causeway in Ireland, the PARCS range presents elements of furniture that can be configured to accommodate intense concentration, teamwork or reflection and escape. In its flexibility, comfort and feel, the system embodies many of the ideas we have advanced in this book. As designer Tom Lloyd explains, 'Too many companies and managers still think that if you are away from your desk, you're not working. It takes an enlightened attitude to recognise that someone sitting on a sofa can also be creating value for the company.'

PARCS modular furniture for knowledge workers designed by Pearson Lloyd for Austrian manufacturer Bene

To help explore how to configure the PARCS system most effectively, the Bene company commissioned Royal College of Art design researcher Catherine Greene to investigate the different character types who inhabit the knowledge economy. Greene's study, *Space For Thought* (2009), presented four typologies which interact with the office in a different way: the 'Anchor' is almost entirely desk based; the 'Connector' moves around a lot within the building; the 'Gatherer' makes regular journeys away from the office but always returns; and the 'Navigator' is rarely in the office at all, working for the organisation at arm's length. It is the complex interactions between these four types that make up the rich tapestry of knowledge work. Interestingly, all four confirmed major problems with concentration and identified key deficiencies in current workspace design.

Breaking with the past

Identifying the type of people who work in your knowledge-based organisation is as important as identifying the type of spaces that will support knowledge work. Are your key people anchored to a workstation, or are they navigating the wider world out there and, as a result, will rarely be physically present in your workplace? It is

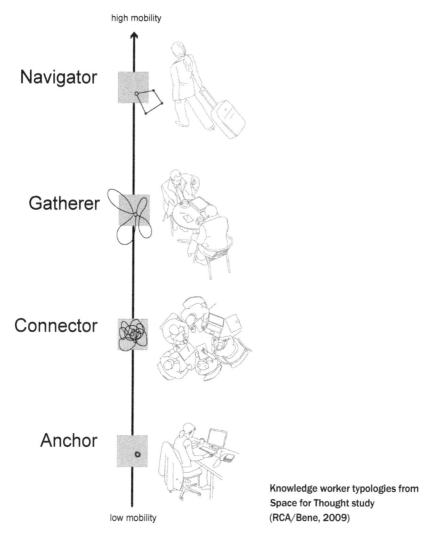

high mobility

Navigator

Gatherer

Connector

Anchor

low mobility

Knowledge worker typologies from
Space for Thought study
(RCA/Bene, 2009)

essential to know. Once you have the right information and insights in place, you can proceed to a design scheme. Here we provide half-a-dozen governing principles on making it happen:

Get leadership from the top: It is the role of the chief executive and other senior directors of the organisation to create the climate for change and publicise successes, and leave the practicalities of implementation to local managers. So ensure there is leadership from the top. This is different from a top-down approach. Bosses who are active and vocal in championing change – but sensitive to local context – will head off most opposition at the pass. The examples we have described of Google in Zurich and Edelman in London clearly illustrate this point.

Test your models at the periphery, not the centre: If you want to pilot new office designs, it is better to test them at the periphery of the organisation first rather than going for it big bang-style at the centre. Take one floor or division or department to model a new style of office environment, as Novartis did with its finance department in Basel. You might seek out the most receptive group of employees to trial the changes, to give yourself the best chance of success. Once the pilot has been well received, the model will be much easier to sell to the rest of the company. A small success can be skillfully publicised and scaled up – a large failure will never be forgotten.

User participation is important: Older knowledge workers are precisely that – experienced and knowledgeable. So make use of their wisdom and expertise. Involve them in a user participation process. Our own research showed us how willing and useful they are in developing design proposals to improve the environment. Such participation needn't involve elaborate methods or cost huge sums of money. User groups, interviews, simple visualisations and rough mock-ups of space all have a part to play. The industrial designer Henry Dreyfuss once wrote: 'When the point of contact between the product and the people becomes a point of friction then the designer has failed.' User participation is essential to minimise the friction.

Support redesign with cultural change: Any substantial office redesign should, wherever possible, be supported by a programme of cultural change for employees. Just as it is missing a trick to introduce a change management scheme for staff without reinforcing its message in the physical design of the workplace, so the opposite is true. Too many companies make the mistake of reconfiguring their environments without proper user engagement to explain how people should behave in the new space. Establishing new protocols of behaviour are essential to ensure that new ways of working take hold within the organisation. The examples we have presented of GlaxoSmithKline Consumer Healthcare's innovation hubs and Pfizer's cross-functional team space illustrate how important cultural change is to office redesign.

Make it inclusive: All knowledge workers have similar requirements from the workspace whatever their age. So make sure your design proposals are inclusive. Targeting senior employees directly with special needs design is unlikely to succeed. It will be viewed as stigmatising and unhelpful and will only serve to widen fissures in organisational culture. It is better to target all employees with better design that will help improve concentration and flow, teamwork and communication, rest and reflection – themes common to all in shared office space.

Go for a radical approach: Finally, don't scale down your ambitions for a better workplace. Ernest Hall, the British entrepreneur who founded the Dean Clough Centre from the dereliction of Halifax's nineteenth century mills, once said that the more audacious the ambition, the more achievable it becomes. Organisations that have compromised to win over reactionary opponents often regret their timidity later. A total revolution is sometimes no more difficult to achieve than a partial one. When, at the dawn of the twentieth century, the advocates of scientific management fatally eroded the status of the nineteenth-century office clerk by removing his high-backed chair and replacing his ornamental desk with modern design, thus introducing supervisory control and undermining a master of his own domain, they really meant business. Similar strength of purpose is required in the early years of the twenty-first century. So, wherever possible, go for a radical approach – and good luck!

20 New demographics, new workspace

Time for change in our approach to office design

When Ronald Reagan became the oldest President of the United States in January 1981 just before his 70th birthday, the White House press corps gathered during his first days in office to ask him how the job was going. The former Hollywood actor, whose self-deprecating wit would help to define his administration, quipped that the hours were long but there was no heavy lifting.

In equating age with the physical ability to work, Reagan was merely echoing a belief system prevalent in the twentieth century – which perceived the value of older people in the workforce to decline in line with their diminishing physical capabilities. But in the twenty-first century, things are already different. Today it is mental capability that increasingly counts and this wisdom and expertise will count even more so tomorrow. Office design, as we have argued, must do more to support this shift – with the 'heavy lifting' in the future being done by architects, designers and developers whose task it will be to create a new workplace paradigm for a new type of workforce.

In this book we have reviewed the ageing of the working population and the rise of the knowledge economy and concluded that the changing workforce requires a new type of workspace – one that accommodates the combination of the natural effects of ageing and the more complex patterns of knowledge work with greater imagination, flexibility and ease. We have examined the barriers to rethinking the culture around older knowledge workers – from IT training to institutional ageism – and proposed ways to redesign the environment to include their needs. In particular we have recommended a mix of settings for concentration, collaboration and contemplation to break up the uniformity of low-choice, low-segmentation open-plan space, which has become so prevalent in recent years as companies have torn down walls to reap the benefits of lower cost and better communication.

In the end, it will be the myriad decisions of business leaders and their designers on the ground that will determine whether the changing workforce gets a different workplace or we go on trying to contain the more fluid patterns of knowledge work within the limited envelope of the familiar office-factory floor. The artist Eugene Delacroix once wrote: 'We work not just to produce, but to give value to time.' In the twenty-first century, that must surely be reflected in our work environments.

References

Anjum, N. (1999) PhD Thesis *'An Environmental Assessment of Office Interiors from Consumers' Perspective'* Duncan of Jordanstone College of Art and Design.

Baty, P. (2007) 'Open-plan Risk to Collegiality' in *The Times Higher* 16 March 2007. http://www.timeshighereducation.co.uk/story.asp?storyCode=208231&sectioncode=26, accessed August 2009.

Becker, F. (2007) 'The Ecology of Knowledge Networks' *California Management Review,* 49(2), pp. 1–20.

Brill, M., Keable, E., and Fabinlak, J. (2000) 'The Myth of the Open Plan' *Journal of Facility Design and Management*, 19, p. 36.

Chartered Institute for Personnel Development (2008) *'Managing the Ageing Workforce: The Role of Total Reward'*. http://www.cipd.co.uk/subjects/dvsequl/agedisc/_agettlrwd.htm, accessed August 2009.

City & Guilds '"Returners" Key to Solving Skills Crisis'. Press Release 18 May 2006. http://www.cityandguilds.com/10944.html.

Corbusier, L. (1946, 2000) *Towards a New Architecture*, New York: Dover Publications Inc.

CROW (Centre for Research into the Older Workforce) (2004) *'Are Older Workers Different*?' April 2004, Briefing Paper 1.

Cranfield School of Management. (2005) *'The Recruitment Confidence Index; Skills Shortages'*, winter 2005. http://www.som.cranfield.ac.uk/som/rci/, accessed August 2009.

Csikszentmihay, M. (1991) Flow*: The Psychology of Optimal Experience*, London: Harper Perennial.

Davenport, T.H., Thomas R.J., and Cantrell, S. (2002) 'The Mysterious Art and Science of Knowledge-Worker Performance' *MIT Sloan Management Review* Fall, pp. 23–30.

Department of Work & Pensions (2006) *Security in Retirement: Towards a New Pension System*, London: The Stationary Office Ltd.

Department of Work & Pensions (2009) *Building a Society for All Ages*, London: The Stationary Office Ltd.

Disability Discrimination Act (1995, 2004) London: The Stationery Office Ltd.

Dreyfuss, H. (1960) *The Measure of Man*, New York: Whitney Library of Design.

Drucker, P. (2001) 'The Next Society: A Survey of the Near Future' *The Economist* November (3).

Drucker, P. (1999) 'Knowledge Worker Productivity: The Biggest Challenge' *California Management Review* 41(Winter), pp. 79–94.

Duffy, F. (2006) Workplace Trends Global Arena Conference, Tate Britain. http://www.workplacetrends.co.uk/2006.html.

Duffy, F. (2008) 'Does the Big Corporate Office have a Future in the UK?' *Building Design Magazine: Office,* December (23).

Dyson, J. (1997) *Against The Odds*, London: Orion.

The Economist (2006) Special Report '*How to Manage an Ageing Workforce: Turning Boomers into Boomerangs*' February 18.

Employment Equality (Age) Regulations (2006) London: The Stationary Office Ltd.

European Commission (Employment & Social Affairs) (2005) Green Paper '*Confronting Demographic Change: A New Solidarity Between Generations*'. http://ec.europa.eu/employment_social/spsi/demographic_challenge_en.htm, accessed August 2009.

Eurostat (2007) '*European Business, Facts and Stats*', Eurostat and European Commission. http://epp.eurostat.ec.europa.eu/portal/page/portal/european_ business/publications/facts_figures, accessed August 2009.

Florida, R. (2002) *The Rise of the Creative Class: And How it's Transforming Work, Leisure, Community and Everyday Life*, New York: Basic Books.

Gofus, N., Conway, S., Kostner, J.,and Cotton, B. (2006) '*Meetings around the World: The Impact of Collaboration on Business Performance*'. Frost & Sullivan White Paper, Frost & Sullivan.

Green, C. (2009) *Space for Thought.* http://www.hhc.rca.ac.uk/2261-2272/all/1/ Space_for_Thought.aspx, accessed September 2009.

Hayutin, A. (2007) 'Global Democratic Shifts' *PREA Quarterly* Fall.

Help the Aged (2005) '*Opportunity Age*'. http://www.policy.helptheaged.org.uk/.../ august_opportunityageresponse.pdf, accessed August 2009.

Illmarinen, J. (1999) '*Ageing Workers in the European Union – Status and Promotion of Work Ability, Employability and Employment*', Helsinki: Finnish Institute of Occupational Health, Ministry of Social Affaire and Health, Ministry of Labour.

The Impact of Office Design on Business Performance (2005) London: CABE & The British Council of Offices.

Johnson, B.C., Manyika, J.M., and Yee, L.A. (2005) 'The Next Revolution in Interactions', *McKinsey Quarterly.* www.mckinseyquarterly.com, accessed August 2009.

Martin, R.L and Moldoveanu, M.C. (2003) 'Capital Versus Talent; The Battle That's Reshaping Business' *Harvard Business Review*, Issue 0307(July 1st).

Morison, R., Erickson, T. and Dychtwald, K. (2006) 'Managing Middlescence' *Harvard Buisness Review* OnPoint edition 3536 (March).

Myerson, J. (2001) *IDEO Masters of Innovation*, London: Laurence King Publishing Ltd.

Myerson, J. (2003) 'The MT Workspace Satisfaction Survey: Workspace Heaven?' *Management Today* 1 June.

Myerson, J. (ed.) (2005) '*Capture It*', London: Royal College of Art Helen Hamlyn Centre.

Myerson, J. and Ross, P. (2006) *Space to Work; New Office Design*, London: Laurence King Publishing Ltd.

'Open Plan or Open Warfare' *The Times Higher* 16 March 2007. http://www.timeshighereducation.co.uk/story.asp?storyCode=208189&sectioncode=26, accessed August 2009.

Organisation for Economic Cooperation and Development (2006) Conference on Globalisation and the Knowledge Economy. http://www.oecd.org/document/54/0,3343,en_2649_34173_37346806_1_1_1_1,00.html, accessed August 2009.

Parsons, T. (2001) 'Headspace: Privacy in Open Plan Offices', Royal College of Art. http://www.hhc.rca.ac.uk/archive/hhrc/programmes/ra/2001/tim.html, accessed August 2009.

Russell, B. and Milmo, C. (2008) 'The Population Timebomb' *The Independent* 22 August 2008.

Skapinker, M. 'Time to be Honest About Open Plan Offices' *The Financial Times* 4 May 2009.

United Nations Programme on Ageing. http://www.un.org/esa/socdev/ageing/madrid_intlplanaction.html.

Whyte, W. (1956) *The Organisation Man*, New York: Doubleday.

Wolfe, T. (1979) *From Bauhaus to Our House*, New York: Bantam.

Index

Note: figures are indicated by bold page numbers.

A

acoustic intervention 91–2, 93–4
age
    changing workforce profile 6–8
    mental characteristics strengthened
      by 28
    and physical changes 67, 69
    rise in median age *12*
    see also older workers; population
      ageing
age discrimination 27
Agora-style workplaces 44
Amsterdam, serviced offices in 114, **114**
Anjum, Nomana 37
Anson, Pascal 126
anthropometrics 48
architecture, modernist 34–5
Arup 109
Australia 15
    see also Welcoming Workplace study

B

Bauhaus 34
Becker, Franklin 87

bed, mini- 126
behavioural norms
    establishing new 132
    for open plan working 105
Bene 130
BMW 31
boredom of mid-career employees 25–6
Bosch & Fjord **113,** 113–14, 123, **124**
brainstorming 116
breakout spaces 121–2
Britain
    demographic trends 13–14
    national income derived from 19
    pension age 16
Building a society for All Ages report 129

C

Camenzind, Stefan 121
Cantrell, Sue 37, 38
Capture It (Harriss and Winstanley) 29–30
Carberry, Neil 13
Centre for Research into the Older
    Workforce (CROW) 27
change in the workplace 7
    cultural 132
    stereotyped expectations of older
      workers 83

China 17
choice **38,** 38–9
choosers 27
Coleman, Chris 121
collaboration
    brainstorming 116
    combined with other spaces 128–9
    and concentration, balance of 22–3,
        61–2
    and concentration framework **64,** 64–5
    design and productivity 36–7
    examples of spaces for 108–18
    Novartis example space for 99–100
    and open plan working 39–41, 118
    principles of space for 118–19, **119**
    segmentation and choice **38,** 38–9
    staff satisfaction and productivity 37–8
communication medium of choice 75–6
concentration
    and collaboration, balance of 22–3,
        61–2
    and collaboration framework **64**
    combined with other spaces 128–9
    cultural artefacts to aid **104,** 104–5
    furniture as aid for 101, **102**
    lighting as aid for 100–1, **101**
    Novartis example space for 99–100

principles of space for 106–7, **107**
    state of flow 102–4, **103**
    Uxus Design example 100–1, **101**
confidential work 65–6
contemplation spaces
    breakout spaces reinstated 121–2
    combined with other spaces 128–9
    domestic space, taking cues from **122,**
        122–3, **123, 124,** 124–6, **125, 126**
    Google, Zurich offices of **120,** 120–1
    principles of space for 126–7, **127**
context, user, importance of 51
control, organisational, and office
    design 32
corporate headquarters 44
Csikszentmihalyi, Mihaly 102–3, **103**
cultural change in the workplace 132

D

Davenport, Thomas 21, 22, 23, 24, 37, 38
Deere & Company 31
demographic trends
    as basis for planning 7
    Britain 13–14
    international responses 17
    Japan 11
    rise in median age *12*

design of offices
    attempts at redesign 22
    attempts at redesigning 22
    to change organisational culture 86–7
    examples of flexible working 42
    influence of Frederick Taylor 33, 34, 43
    leadership from the top 131
    machines, offices as 33–4
    older workers' requirements 29–30
    principles for 131–3
    radical approach as better 132–3
    redesign as priority for older workers 9–10
    for rest and recuperation 70–1
    and staff satisfaction 37–8
    and state of flow **104,** 104–5, **105**
    testing at the peripheral 132
    three generic types of workplace 98
    three waves of 43
    user context, importance of 51
    user participation 132
    see also inclusive design
desk postbox 105
deteriorating dependency ratio 14
development for older workers 26

Disability Discrimination Acts (1995 and 2004) 15
disabled workers, stigmatisation of in design 48–9
discrimination, age 27, 80–2
domestic space, taking cues from **122,** 122–6, **123, 124, 125, 126**
Dreyfuss, Henry 48, 51
Drucker, Peter 18, 19, 20
Duffy, Frank 36, 43–4
Dychtwald, Ken 25
Dyson, James 116–18, **117**

E
Edelman **109,** 109–10
Employment Equality (Age) Regulations (2006) 15
environments designed for research 57–8, 91–8
ergonomics 50
Erickson, Tamara 25
Europe
    knowledge economy in 19
    percentage knowledge workers in workforce **18**
eyesight 49

F

Finland 28–9
fitness for work of older workers 67
flexible working
    examples of office design 42
    location 44–5
    networked office 43–4
    novelty approaches, impact of 45–6
    workstation utilisation 42–3
flow, state of
    optimal experience of 102–3, **103**
    and workplace design **104,** 104–5, **105**
Freeman Centre, Sussex University 40–1
From Bauhaus to Our House (Wolfe) 34
functional ability, loss of 50
furniture
    as aid to concentration 101, **102**
    alternative 92, 94–6
    for collaboration 113–14
    designed for knowledge workers 130,
      130

G

Gall, Joseph G. 102
garden, mini- 126
Germany 17, 19

giant whiteboards 113
GlaxoSmithKline Consumer Healthcare
    110–11, **111**
Google, Zurich offices of 120–1
government policy 15–17, 129
Greene, Catherine 130
guild-like workspaces 44

H

Hall, Ernest 132–3
Harriss, Harriet 29
Hazard, Maria 112
headquarters, corporate 44
Headspace: Privacy in Open Plan Offices
    (Parsons) 104–5
health and well-being
    design for 50–1
    fitness for work 67
    see also contemplation spaces
hearing 49
Hemingway, Wayne 125, **125**
home-working 45, 62–3, 64
hot-desking 39, 63–4, 64
hoteling 39

I

IDEO 114–16, **115**

Ilmarinen, Juhani 28

Impact of Office Design on Business Performance, The (Duffy) 36–7

inclusive design
  benefits for all ages 97
  as general principle 132
  for health and well-being 50–1
  initial developments 47–8
  physical requirements for older workers 49–50
  reaction against one-size-fits-all 48–9
  responsibility on employers/designers 49

India 17

information technology
  ability to access 75
  alternatives to screen-based working 78–9
  communication medium of choice 75–6
  ineffective deployment of 23–4
  need for alternatives 77–8
  older workers' requirements 30
  perception of older workers concerning 72
  self-sufficiency, problems with 74–5

training in 73–4

innovation
  brainstorming 116
  consultancies 114–16, **115**
  hubs 110–11, **111**
  open plan working for 116–18, **117**

International Plan on Ageing (United Nations) 17

Interpolis 128–9, **129**

interviews conducted for research 57

Ireland 19

J

Jackson, Betty 105–6

Japan 11
  see also Welcoming Workplace study

jugglers 27

K

Kinder 126

Kline, Roger 41

knowledge work(ers)
  application of term to roles 18–19
  attempts at workplace design for 22
  Australia 15
  boredom in mid-career 25–6
  characteristics of 21

collaboration/concentration balance 22–3
furniture designed for 130, **130**
as hard to manage for 20–1
ineffective deployment of IT for 23–4
national income derived from 19, **19**
older workers 9
and organisation of work 8–9
percentage in European workforce **18**
tacit interactions 20
typology of 130–1
Kohler, Mervyn 13

L
Le Corbusier 34
leadership development for older workers 26
leadership from the top 131
legislation 15
life expectancy 12
lighting conditions 49, 92, 94, 100–1, 114, 119
Lloyd, Tom 130
locations, working in different 44–5
Lodge-style working 45

M
Macquarie 112–13
Mason, Mark 109
Measure of Man, The (Dreyfuss) 48, 51
meeting tree 112–13, **113**
mental capacity
changes with age 50
importance of 134
mentoring schemes 26
Mexx International **122,** 122–3, **123**
mid-career workers
boredom of 25–6
revitalisation of careers 26
'middle-age' countries 14
middlescence 25–6
mini-bed/garden 126
Modern Movement 32, 33–5
Moggridge, Bill 115–16
Momentum **113,** 113–14, 123, **124**
Monsanto 40
Morey Smith, Linda 108–9
Morison, Robert 25
muscular-skeletal disorders 69

N

natural interventions 93
networked office 43–4
Nilsson, Ann-Charlotte 101
Nishizawa, Ryue 123
no door mat 105
noise in the office 62
Nokia 108, **108**
Novartis 99–100

O

office design
    attempts at redesigning 22
    to change organisational culture 86–7
    examples of flexible working 42
    future of 90–1
    influence of Frederick Taylor 33, 34,
        43
    leadership from the top 131
    machines, offices as 33–4
    Modern Movement 32, 33–5
    and organisational control 32
    principles for 131–3
    radical approach as better 132–3
    for rest and recuperation 70–1
    and staff satisfaction 37–8
    and state of flow **104,** 104–5, **105**

testing at the peripheral 132
three generic types of workplace 98
three waves of 43
user context, importance of 51
user participation 132
    see also inclusive design
older workers
    ability to access IT 75
    alternatives to screen-based working
        78–9
    ambivalence towards in companies
        80–2
    attitudes concerning technology 72–3
    boredom of 25–6
    communication medium of choice
        75–6
    concentration in open plan offices
        61–2
    design requirements of 29–30
    discrimination against 27
    examples of adaptation to 31
    fitness for work 67
    health and well-being, design for 50–1
    home-working 62–3
    and IT training 73–4
    mental characteristics of 28
    need for alternatives to IT 77–8

and noise in the office 62
and open plan working 60–2, 69–70
perception of concerning IT 72
physical requirements for 49–50
reluctance to express needs 84
research into needs of, importance of
    54–5
revitalisation of careers 26
self-sufficiency, problems with 74–5
sensitivity to physical environment
    67–8
stereotyped expectations of 83
stigmatisation of in design 48–9
'oldest' countries 14
one-size-fits-all design, reaction against
    48–9
open plan working
    behaviour norms for 105
    collaboration as suffering from 118
    collaboration/concentration balance
        61–2
    and confidential work 65–6
    encountered during research 59–60
    home-working as alternative 62–3
    for innovation 116–18, **117**
    lack of control over environment of 68
    need for alternatives to sitting 68–9

and older workers 60–2
    problems with 39–41, 65–6, 69–70
    reasons for 39, 65
Opportunity Age white paper 15–16
organisational control and office design 32
organisational ecology 87

P

PARCS furniture range 130, **130**
Parsons, Tim 104–5
Peach, Sevil 99, 100, 114, 122, 123
Pearson Lloyd 130
pension age
    expectancy of working past 16–17
    increases in 11–12, 16
pensions 16
permeable privacy artefacts 105
Peters, Tom 116
Pfizer 111–12
Philips, Robert 110
physical requirements for older workers
    49–50
planning, demographic trends as basis
    for 7
policy, government 15–17, 129
population ageing
    Australia 15

Britain 13–14
    as challenge to national wealth 8
    globally 14–15
    international responses 17
    Japan 11
principles
    of design 131–3
    of space for collaboration 118–19,
        119
    of space for concentration 106–7,
        107
    of space for contemplation 126–7,
        127
privacy artefacts 105
productivity of knowledge workers
    and design 36–7
    issues affecting 22–4
    lack of knowledge on how to improve
        37–8
    and screen-based working 79
    and staff satisfaction 37–8
professional clustering 44
Project Ignite 110–11
project space 118–19, **119**

Q
quality of life at work 125–6

R
radical approach to design 132–3
recuperation
    design for 70–1
    need for 126
    need for alternatives to sitting 68–70
    see also contemplation spaces
research into older peoples' needs
    ambivalence towards older workers
        80–2
    collaboration/concentration framework
        64, 64–5
    environments designed for 57–8, 91–8
    fitness for work 67–8
    hot-desking 63–4
    identifying needs 84
    importance of 54–5
    interviews conducted 57
    multidisciplinary approach 55–6
    multinational focus 56–7
    older workers and open plan working
        60–2
    open plan working 68–70
    open plan working seen 59–60
    rest and recuperation, design for 70–1
    stereotyped expectations of older
        workers 83

summary of findings 86
technology and older workers 72–9
rest and recuperation
    design for 70–1
    need for 126
    see also contemplation spaces
retirement age
    expectancy of working past 16–17
    increases in 11–12, 16
revitalisation of careers 26

S
sabbaticals 26
satisfaction of staff and productivity 37–8
scientific management 33, 34–5
Security in Retirement: Towards a New
    Pensions System white paper 16
segmentation **38,** 38–9
Sejima, Kazuyo 123
serviced offices 114, **114**
social democratic office 43
Space for Thought (Greene) 130–1, **131**
special needs design 48–9
staff satisfaction and productivity 37–8
state of flow
    optimal experience of 102–3, **103**
    and workplace design **104,** 104–5, **105**

stigmatisation in design 48–9
survivors 27
Sussex University 40–1

T
tacit jobs 20
Taylor, Frederick 33, 43
teamwork. *see* collaboration
technology
    ability to access 75
    alternatives to screen-based working
        78–9
    communication medium of choice
        75–6
    ineffective deployment of 23–4
    intervention 92, 94
    need for alternatives 77–8
    older workers' requirements 30
    perception of older workers concerning
        72
    self-sufficiency, problems with 74–5
    training in 73–4
Thomas, Bob 37, 38
Towards a New Architecture (Le
    Corbusier) 34
Toyota 31
training for older workers 26

transactional work 20
transformational jobs 19–20

U
umbrella chair **104,** 105
United Nations International Plan on
    Ageing 17
United States 19
users
    context of as important 51
    participation of in design 132
Uxus Design 100–1, **101**

V
Veldhoen + Co 128, **129**

W
Welcoming Workplace study
    ambivalence towards older workers
        80–2
    collaboration/concentration framework
        64, 64–5
    environments designed for 57–8, 91–8
    fitness for work 67–8
    hot-desking 63–4
    identifying older peoples' needs 84
    interviews conducted 57

multidisciplinary approach 55–6
multinational focus 56–7
need for alternatives to sitting 68–70
need for research 54–5
older workers and open plan working
    60–2, 68–70
open plan working seen 59–60
rest and recuperation, design for 70–1
stereotyped expectations of older
    workers 83
summary of findings 86
technology and older workers 72–9
well-being and health, design for 50–1
    see also contemplation spaces
white papers
    Opportunity Age 15–16
    Security in Retirement: Towards a New
        Pensions System 16
whiteboards, giant 113
Wilkinson, Clive 112–13
Winstanley, Suzi 29
Wolfe, Tom 34
Work Ability 28–9
work ethic and office design 33
workforce, age-balance in the UK 13–14
workplace
    change in 7

knowledge work in 8–9
quality of life at 125–6
workplace design
attempts at redesigning 22
to change organisational culture 86–7
examples of flexible working 42
leadership from the top 131
principles for 131–3
radical approach as better 132–3
and staff satisfaction 37–8
and state of flow **104,** 104–5, **105**
testing at the peripheral 132
three generic types of workplace 98
user context, importance of 51
user participation 132
see also inclusive design
workstation utilisation 42–3

Y
'young' countries 15